THE
FAMILY-POWERED
CHURCH

by Pamela J. Erwin

Loveland, Colorado

To my parents,
Trulon and Frances Creel,
who taught me what family should be.

Visit our Web site: **www.grouppublishing.com**

Credits
    Editor: John J. Fanella
    Creative Development Editor: Dave Thornton
    Chief Creative Officer: Joani Schultz
    Copy Editor: Pam Klein
    Art Director: Randy Kady
    Cover Art Director: Jeff A. Storm
    Cover Designer: Alan Furst, Inc.
    Cover Photography: FPG International, Stone, and SuperStock, Inc.
    Computer Graphic Artists: Dana Sherrer and Tracy K. Donaldson
    Production Manager: Peggy Naylor

ISBN 0-7644-2093-3

10 9 8 7 6 5 4 3 2 1   09 08 07 06 05 04 03 02 01 00

Printed in the United States of America.

CONTENTS

FOREWORD

THE POSTMODERN CHURCH IS FACING a looming crisis of inconceivable magnitude. This crisis is the result of the subtle yet sweeping decision to shift the church's primary task from building a strong, vibrant faith community that is called, empowered, and equipped to serve a lost, broken world to developing a programmatic structure that separates and segments the church into small, generationally homogeneous, unconnected factions in order to keep pace with the Jones' church down the street.

Fragmentation is the most apt description of the postmodern church. After years of striving for perceived programmatic excellence and trying to inaugurate a church growth strategy that "consumers" will respond to, we have allowed the proverbial programmatic tail to wag the dog. The church has become a programmatic shell around which the various other ministries of the church loosely orbit.

On any given Sunday, a family of five will arrive and disperse into separate rooms to take part in various educational or worship experiences that are rarely philosophically, or even strategically, connected. Then, following the lesson or service, they all climb into the minivan and drive home, with virtually no relational or spiritual family connection. And what about the single mother who works all week to make ends meet and to get her kids "into" church (i.e., they like it) while she tries to find a place of personal safety and comfort? She will generally arrive alone, sit alone, and go home, without anyone asking how she is doing or offering support.

The fragmented church hurts even the healthiest, most "together" family as well as the nontraditional family that needs support. The programmatic segmentation in today's churches leaves healthy families on their own to find time for intimate Christian community and worship. It leaves single people trying to somehow fit in with others of like status, and it leaves divorced and single-parent families struggling from a lack of meaningful support.

Is this what God intends for us?

Pamela Erwin does not think so, and neither do I. In the church today, we need all the help we can get to begin to heal the fractures of the programmatic church. We need to rediscover our theology of the local church. We need to take an honest look at where we are failing our nuclear families and those in the congregation who are not connected to others. We need to rediscover what it means to be a family of families.

This book is a must-read for those who care about the people in the local church. For the leadership—pastors, elders, deacons, staff, and laity—this book will be a valuable tool for years to come. There are practical suggestions and broad theological challenges. For the church that recognizes the need to change, *The Family-Powered Church* can be used as a planning tool for a leadership retreat or strategic planning team or as a teaching tool for new leaders on a ministry team.

The need is urgent, the issues are real, and the task is enormous, but Pamela Erwin offers great insight and wisdom in calling us back to being the church as God intends—a community of believers who care for one another.

Chap Clark, Ph.D.
Associate Professor of Youth and Family Ministry,
Fuller Theological Seminary
Executive Administrator, Glendale Presbyterian Church

INTRODUCTION

WRITING THIS BOOK HAS BEEN the culmination of a long journey into discovering the meaning of family and church. When I first entered youth ministry, I thought the focus would naturally be on adolescents. I intended to fill my days planning lock-ins and retreats, leading Bible studies, and spending time with teens. What I discovered, however, was that teenagers do not live in a vacuum. If I wanted to have long-term, far-reaching effects in teenagers' lives and for the kingdom, my ministry had to include the family.

For the past few years I have been teaching a course to graduate students entitled Youth Ministry and the Family. The students and I spend a significant portion of our class time discussing the subject of ministering to families. "What is the most effective way for churches to reach families?" "What is family ministry?" "How do we do it?" The results of these discussions, together with my own personal experiences, are presented in the pages of this book.

I recently spoke with a friend who has been ministering to families and youth for more than twenty years and who has an obvious passion for families and for the church. I was seeking his wisdom and counsel as I sorted through my own research and thoughts for this book. We discussed ways that churches might minister to families more effectively and what the needs of today's families are. I also asked him what he felt was the biggest issue facing churches in their ministries to families. He said, "In most churches in America today, the ministries are detrimental to families. I call it 'fragmentation of the family by design.'"

As I processed my friend's comment, I realized that he was accurate in his assessment. Most of what we do in our churches, even when we call it family ministry, serves to disrupt, disconnect, and divide families. Through this book, I hope those of us in ministry will begin to think differently—to not only change the way we *do* ministry, but to change the way we *think about* ministry.

This is a book about creating community within the church. A recent article in Christianity Today noted that "community" is now the most popular designation in church names.[1] Changing the name of a church will not automatically create a sense of community, though.

Part 1 looks at family ministry and what it means to be a church community—a family of families—including discussing the theological and philosophical understandings of community, family, and church.

Part 2 discusses components vital to healthy families and healthy churches: story and ritual. The chapters in this section highlight the ways in which story and ritual, including rites of passage, bring a depth and richness to churches and families.

Part 3 is a practical section, providing an in-depth look at the vital connections families need and ways that churches can help families make those connections. The final chapter offers practical research tips to help you better understand the needs of families in your community.

As family ministry continues to emerge, my hope is that this book will serve as a road map, leading you not only to family ministry, but to creating a family of families within the church.

References
1. Ken Walker, "Church Name-Dropping Pays Off," Christianity Today (June 14, 1999), 15.

PART ONE:
FOUNDATIONS STRENGTHEN FAMILY MINISTRY

DEFINING
FAMILY MINISTRY

C H A P T E R   O N E

RECENTLY I SPOKE WITH A SENIOR PASTOR at a workshop on family ministry. His schedule was very full, but he managed to set aside a day away from his church to attend the workshop. He wanted a bag full of family ministry "tricks" to implement when he got home. His comment to me was revealing: "Just tell me what to do and I'll do it. I don't have time to think!" By the end of the workshop, however, this pastor changed his mind. He realized that family ministry is not something that can be photocopied from one church and used by another. It's more organic than that; it's a way of thinking, a theological conviction, and a philosophy. It's not simply a program to be modeled.

Along with small groups and seeker services, family ministry is one of the top ministry concerns pastors and lay leaders express in light of today's shifting cultural tides. But just what is family ministry? In preparation for this book, a group of graduate students and I talked to pastors from more than twenty churches in

> *Family ministry is not something that can be photocopied from one church and used by another. It's more organic than that; it's a way of thinking, a theological conviction, and a philosophy. It's not simply a program to be modeled.*

North America and gathered more than one hundred surveys from church leaders across the United States. Their comments and questions reflect the common confusion about family ministry:

- Family ministry is a desire of my heart, but I have no direction or clue how to get there.
- Family ministry? It doesn't exist. The families hit the church doors and scatter.
- How do we do family ministry without excluding singles and senior adults?
- Church seems to be in conflict with family time and activities.
- Family ministry is badly needed! The body of Christ is dying without it.

In addition, family ministry must build a network of healthy families. Family ministry is about building the church into a "family of families," not just strengthening individual families. Family ministry might be defined as follows: Family ministry is the church-supported effort to build a network of strong, healthy, and happy families. A church that practices family ministry based on this definition is a family-powered church.

WHY WE NEED FAMILY-POWERED CHURCHES

THE FAMILY IS IN TROUBLE AND NEEDS THE CHURCH

There is no doubt that the family is in trouble. Research on attitudes and behavior that affect the family unit consistently demonstrates that as a society we are dismantling the institution of family. Increasing divorce rates, never-married single people encouraged by society to have children on their own, and unmarried couples having children are just a few examples of what is happening in our world. Historical social rules have been tossed aside and have been replaced by a value system based on personal preference and ideology.

This breakdown of the meaning and form of the family brings devastating consequences. Children are now left to fend for themselves at a young age. Parents are stressed, and marriages are in trouble. People are running as fast as they can. In this hectic world, little time remains for intimacy, relationships, or family.

Adding to this frustration, society tells parents that they should be able to do it all without support from outside the nuclear family. The societal support systems of extended family and community networks are no longer available to many families. As a result, many families are isolated and alone. They need support but believe they are failing because they cannot keep it all together on their own.

The church is ideally suited to step into this void. People are tired, lonely, and in need of connections. Many, if not most, families have neither the energy nor the resources to create an environment of peace and safety within the context of the family. People are desperate for closeness; for relational warmth and intimacy; and

The family is in trouble and needs what the church has to offer—a community.

for love, fellowship, and meaning. The family is in trouble and needs what the church has to offer—a community.

THE CHURCH RARELY FUNCTIONS AS A COMMUNITY

Many churches focus on programs in an attempt to make their ministry more effective. However, programs can result in a rugged individualism not dissimilar to historical America. People need each other; yet so often churches seek to draw in people by appealing to their individual tastes and feelings and by treating them as if they were completely independent.

Today's typical church offers children's ministries, youth ministries, senior adult ministries, men's ministries, women's ministries, and ministries centered around various felt needs such as divorce and recovery. Many of these ministries function as autonomous units within the context of the larger church body. The problem with programs targeted at individuals is that they have taken their toll on healthy, intimate relationships in both the church and the family. Dennis Guernsey, in *A New Design for Family Ministry*, writes, "If we preach a gospel that neglects the welfare of the whole in exchange for the happiness of the individual, then the Church as a living, pulsing body is weakened as is the welfare of the family. We must recover the priority of interrelationship."[1]

The church must recall the new command Jesus gave his disciples: "Love one another" (John 13:34). This is the essence of what it means to live as the church. When we allow ourselves to be swept up in thinking that the church is about programs, educational opportunities, musical and rhetorical entertainment, and appealing to every individual's tastes, we lose our main focus. Jesus called the church to be a family of families. Today the church more often resembles a corporation or a mall of specialty shops than a family.

Jesus called the church to be a family of families. Today the church more often resembles a corporation or a mall of specialty shops than a family.

MOST FAMILIES WHO NEED HELP DO NOT TURN TO THE CHURCH UNTIL IT IS TOO LATE

Many churches see family ministry as the department that offers educational opportunities and programs. It's no surprise that in most churches the people who show up at such events are those who need them the least. Take the typical parenting seminar, for example. The parents who are least involved with their children are the ones least likely to attend. These programs do have value, but the key people these programs need to reach rarely have sufficient relational trust in the strangers at church to actually attend. As odd as it may seem, people do not always feel safe at church. When it comes to sharing the intimate details of one's life, *especially* when a person is struggling with a problem, church-sponsored programs and classes may be frightening. Some may even avoid these types of events because they don't want to open themselves up to what they perceive to be more guilt by coming to hear what they already intuitively know.

The church must redefine itself as a community of families—families that are intimately connected to one another. Before people can be expected to benefit from (or even attend) classes, programs, and events, the church must create an environment of relational safety, warmth, and connectedness. Without this, the fellowship is hollow and superficial.

FAMILY MINISTRY IS MORE THAN PROGRAMS AND EDUCATIONAL OPPORTUNITIES

In light of the fact that not everyone feels connected to the church community, the church's mission must be to care for and connect with every family in the church, not just families that show up to "family ministry" events. This is the key to a family-powered church: it is less about what we *do* than it is about who we *are*. The doing follows the being.

Most books, courses, and articles on family ministry fall back on the idea that we can meet the family needs of people by offering more to do. But rarely do churches have the courage to cancel programs and ministries as fast as they have added them. Today the biggest problem for the average church is not that they have too few activities and programs, but that they have far too many!

> *Family ministry is less about what we* do *than it is about who we* are. *The doing follows the being.*

Family ministry, then, is more about *how* and *why* we do what we do than it is about providing programs and ministries. Churches committed to building a family-powered church must focus on functioning in relational terms as a family rather than on adding to the busyness of already harried church members.

FAMILY MINISTRY IS A *WAY OF THINKING* THAT AFFECTS EVERY ASPECT OF THE CHURCH'S STRUCTURE, PROGRAMS, AND MINISTRY

Family ministry is a comprehensive thinking process. It is not limited to a single department, staff member, or to the nuclear family. Rather, it's a unifying purpose that encompasses all areas of ministry. It is vital that churches understand this fundamental nature of family ministry.

Any church that seeks to be a family of families, anchored by a theology, vision, and philosophy of ministry, continually returns to one question: Does what we do *match what we believe, as well as who we* are?

Any church that seeks to be a family of families, anchored by a theology, vision, and philosophy of ministry, continually returns to one question: Does what we *do* match what we *believe*, as well as who we *are*? When church leaders have the courage to examine programs in light of that question, taking a critical look at even the sacred-cow programs and ministries, a family-powered church will begin to take root.

FAMILY MINISTRY IS NOT AN OPTION TO BE DEBATED, BUT AN ESSENTIAL ELEMENT OF CHURCH LIFE

"The church of the first century was called to leave their earthly familial allegiances and to bond to one another as the new family of God. The revolutionary impact of the first-century church was their love for one another as Christ had commanded them. The need for the church in the twentieth century is to respond as they responded. *We are the Church and we are family.* Let us get on with our business" [emphasis added].[2]

Far too often church growth strategies overemphasize numbers and eclipse the church's real purpose: people being connected to and loving others in the name of Jesus Christ. This connection must first take place in the home, but then it must spill over into relationships in the church. Intimacy in the church must be a natural, close, and real extension of intimacy in the Christian household.

Jack and Judith Balswick, authors of *The Family: A Christian Perspective on the Contemporary Home*, capture the essence of the church's relational purpose: "The church, then, is to be a family to families, and a source of identity and support for isolated nuclear families. The church needs to become a community of faith...[where it] must avoid the pitfall of exclusivity and the tendency to accept only certain types of people."[3]

This is the ultimate goal of a family-powered church—every single person is known, loved, and empowered for ministry. Empowering means helping each person recognize his or her strengths and potential and providing appropriate opportunities to use them. As individuals begin to connect with others in the bond of the Spirit, whole new possibilities for ministry, expression of gifts, and creativity are realized.

As individuals begin to connect with others in the bond of the Spirit, whole new possibilities for ministry, expression of gifts, and creativity are realized.

Thus God's people are built into the kind of temple that brings him glory and honor, demonstrating to the world that God lives through his church.

By becoming aware of the need for a family-powered church, your church is taking the first step toward becoming one. A thought process this sweeping will not be adopted or perfected overnight. But realizing the true nature and extent of family ministry is half the challenge. I encourage you to reread this chapter, making sure that you have a clear picture of family ministry. As you assimilate this vision, hear the words of the Apostle Paul as he speaks of the beauty of family ministry:

"For through him we both have access to the Father by one Spirit. Consequently, you are no longer foreigners and aliens, but fellow citizens with God's people and members of God's household, built on the foundation of the apostles and prophets, with Christ Jesus himself as the chief cornerstone. In him the whole building is joined together and rises to become a holy temple in the Lord. And in him you too are being built together to become a dwelling in which God lives by his Spirit" (Ephesians 2:18-22).

References

1. Dennis B. Guernsey, *A New Design for Family Ministry* (Elgin, IL: David C. Cook Publishing, 1982), 99.
2. Dennis B. Guernsey, *A New Design for Family Ministry*, 112.
3. Jack O. Balswick and Judith K. Balswick, *The Family: A Christian Perspective on the Contemporary Home* (Grand Rapids, MI: Baker Book House, 1991, 1999), 304.

AUTHENTICATING
FAMILY MINISTRY

CHAPTER TWO

FAMILY MINISTRY MUST REST FIRMLY on a solid theological, vision-ary, and philosophical foundation. When implementing new ways of thinking about ministry, church life, and programming, many churches either ignore or only casually attempt to build a theological basis for ministry. The danger of this kind of negligence is that such churches could actually be out of sync with the ministry mandates of Scripture. We must ensure that what is done in the name of God and the church lines up with what Scripture teaches.

CREATING A THEOLOGICAL
FOUNDATION OF FAMILY MINISTRY

A church seeking to become a family-powered church should begin by developing a theology of church and family life that is true to Scripture and yet addresses the uniqueness of that particular ministry. Such a the-ology addresses questions ranging from "Is the church to be an intimate, connected gathering of all the members?" to "Is it sufficient for each family system to be connected to two or three other family systems?" Following are other questions that may arise:

- Is it important for the local church to connect people who come from different life situations?
- Do single people need to feel close to families for the church to be an authentic community?
- How do programs fit with our theology of church life, family life, and community life?

A theology of family ministry integrates three categories: a theology of church life (or relationships in the church), a theology of family, and a theology of family ministry. Such a theology plays an important role in

- helping the church remember what it is called both to do and be;
- creating an objective, external source of authority in resolving disputes and/or misunderstandings; and
- allowing the church to remain theologically grounded in a world that is rapidly changing.

To lay the groundwork for the development of a theology of family ministry, six areas must be seriously considered.

FOR EVERY INDIVIDUAL, THE RELATIONSHIP WITH GOD IS PRIMARY

Jesus makes no apology when he calls for loyalty to God above any other form of relational allegiance when he states, "If anyone comes to me and does not hate his father and mother, his wife and children, his brothers and sisters—yes, even his own life—he cannot be my disciple" (Luke 14:26). Some use this passage to say that Jesus did not consider the nuclear family important in God's plan. Advocates of this position point out that the church's task is to both be and provide for that place of relational loyalty in the local gathering of believers called the church.

> *Jesus makes no apology when he calls for loyalty to God above any other form of relational allegiance.*

However, Jesus' statement has nothing to do with other human relationships or how we prioritize our lives as people who live, work, and worship together. Rather, he calls us to be radically loyal to him as the Son of God and to make that loyalty the primary guiding principle in our relationships. Every person desiring to be a disciple of Jesus must make that relationship central in his or her relationships.

WHEN IT COMES TO HUMAN RELATIONSHIPS, THERE IS NO TIGHTER BOND THAN MARRIAGE

The Bible has much to say about how people are to function in relationships. In particular, husbands and wives are called to the closest possible union of hearts, minds, and souls. For example,

> • Jesus spoke about the intimacy of marriage when he used a carpenter's term for "glue together" in describing the relationship between a husband and wife: "Haven't you read," he replied, "that at the beginning the Creator 'made them male and female,' and said, 'For this reason a man will leave his father and mother and be united to his wife, and the two will become one flesh'? So they are no longer two, but one. Therefore what God has *joined together*, let man not separate" (Matthew 19:4-6, emphasis added).
>
> • Solomon's Song of Songs 5:16b describes the relationship between a husband and wife in joyful, intimate terms: "This is my lover, this my friend."
>
> • In Genesis 2:18 God created Eve because Adam needed a "helper." The Hebrew word for helper used here is *ezer*, and it is used in the Old Testament to refer to God as the ultimate helper (except for a few men who are actually named Ezer). In other words, when God created Eve as a complement to Adam, he intended her to come alongside of Adam as a relational partner. Adam and Eve were to be mutual helpers as the two moved through life together.
>
> • The apparent role differences between men and women in Ephesians 5:22-33 seem to be contingent upon verse 21, "Submit to one another out of reverence for Christ." Mutual submission in love and service is an important aspect of a theology of marriage.

The Bible's emphasis on the special and divine role of marriage cannot be underestimated. Among all of our human relationships, marriage is the one relationship to which God has attached unique blessing and, consequently, unique demands. A family-powered church should do all it can to support couples in living out the marriage covenant.

THE NURTURING OF CHILDREN IS CONNECTED TO THE COVENANT OF MARRIAGE

In human relationships marriage takes precedence, even over the relationship with children. However, when children enter a family, the couple must place them at the top of their joint list of relational loyalties. Although this is not explicitly spelled out in Scripture, it is implied throughout. The central passage that shows how important parents are is the fifth commandment (Exodus 20:12): "Honor your father and your mother, so that you may live long in the land the Lord your God is giving you." This command demonstrates that the parents are another high-priority human relationship in God's plan. Not only is it

Among all of our human relationships, marriage is the one relationship to which God has attached unique blessing and, consequently, unique demands.

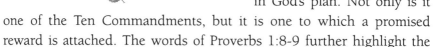

one of the Ten Commandments, but it is one to which a promised reward is attached. The words of Proverbs 1:8-9 further highlight the benefits of honoring parents: "Listen, my son, to your father's instruction and do not forsake your mother's teaching. They will be a garland to grace your head and a chain to adorn your neck."

EXTENDED FAMILY REMAINS A HIGH PRIORITY AFTER CHILDREN

Although Jesus' statement in Luke 14:26 seems to imply that, especially at this third level of loyalty and priority, the extended family is not as important as the church, the New Testament does suggest that we have a kinship responsibility to our extended family relations. We see this principle in situations such as when

• Peter asks the Lord to heal his mother-in-law (which Jesus does, see Mark 1:30-31).

• Paul tells Timothy that families should take responsibility for their own relatives if they are able: "If any woman who is a believer has widows in her family, she should help them and not let the church be burdened with them, so that the church can help those widows who are really in need" (1 Timothy 5:16).

Such biblical examples demonstrate that our extended families also deserve our attention.

RELATIONSHIPS ARE AT THE CENTER OF WHAT IT MEANS TO FUNCTION AS THE CHURCH

Thinking again on Jesus' new command in John 13:34 to "Love one another. As I have loved you…" we see that a new order of intimate relationships marked by love is what the New Testament church understood to be the heart of the Christian experience. Jesus went so far as to say, "By this all men will know that you are my disciples, if you love one another" (John 13:35).

In Ephesians 4:32–5:2, Paul continues Jesus' emphasis on relational love, writing to the Ephesians to "be kind and compassionate to one another, forgiving each other, just as in Christ God forgave you."

In Galatians 5:14-15, Paul takes a different approach to the church being founded on love and intimacy by describing the consequences of factions and infighting: "The entire law is summed up in a single command: 'Love your neighbor as yourself.' If you keep on biting and devouring each other, watch out or you will be destroyed by each other."

And in 1 John 3:11 and 16-18, John reminds the believers that love is the most important issue in the body of Christ: "This is the message you heard from the beginning: We should love one another…This is how we know what love is: Jesus Christ laid down his life for us. And we ought to lay down our lives for our brothers. If anyone has material possessions and sees his brother in need but has no pity on him, how can the love of God be in him? Dear children, let us not love with words or tongue but with actions and in truth."

The church is intended to be a family. Note how John uses "brother" and refers to the church as "dear children." Jesus also affirms the church as a family. When someone told Jesus that his mother and brothers were looking for him, "He replied to him, 'Who is my mother and who are my brothers?' Pointing to his disciples, he said, 'Here are my mother and my brothers. For whoever does the will of my Father in heaven is my brother and sister and mother'" (Matthew 12:48-50). On the surface this is not a very comforting passage for those who seek a biblical rationale for the support of the nuclear family. Elsewhere Scripture points to a priority of relational commitment and loyalty that begins in the marriage relationship, extends to children, and continues toward support of extended family relations. So what does Jesus mean? Is this a contradiction of the rest of Scripture? Not at all! Jesus is not negating family relationships but describing Christian relationships in family terms.

In 1 Thessalonians 2, Paul affirms to the church his commitment of love and caring. Throughout this passage, he describes his ministry in family terms. "But we were gentle among you, like a mother caring for her little children…we dealt with each of you as a father deals with his own children" (verses 7, 11). Paul views his relationship to the Thessalonian church as one of a loving family member.

Similarly, Paul instructs Timothy to treat those in his church as family. "Do not rebuke an older man harshly, but exhort him as if he were your father. Treat younger men as brothers, older women as mothers, and younger women as sisters, with absolute purity" (1 Timothy 5:1-2). The understanding is that our relationships in the church are to be close and intimate—as our family relationships are.

Some reject the notion of "church as a family" in an attempt to defend the primacy of the marriage and family relationships. As Rodney Clapp contends in *Families at the Crossroads: Beyond Traditional and Modern Options,* "we cannot put Jesus first and still put family first."[1] The fact is that Jesus called his followers to a new and radical form of intimacy, loyalty, and allegiance that was unheard of outside of kinship relations. His call to "love one another as I have loved you" leaves little room for fellowship among relationally distant acquaintances.

The church is not a place, a gathering, a club, or even a worshipping congregation. The church is called to be an intimate family in which each member is equally loved and valued. As Charles Sell writes in *Family Ministry,*

> *The church is not a place, a gathering, a club, or even a worshipping congregation. The church is called to be an intimate family in which each member is equally loved and valued.*

"[From the New Testament we can conclude that] there is clearly a kindly, personal relating in the church. A corporate, superficial expression of love and responsibility cannot possibly qualify for the intimate expressions of the church family seen in the New Testament. All of the close, dynamic aspects of family life are to be found in the church body: cherishing, caring, encouraging, rebuking, confessing, repenting, confronting, forgiving, expressing kindness, and communicating honestly...Church life and family life are closely interrelated in New Testament experience. The dynamic relationship between the two is so obvious that it appears to be taken for granted by the New Testament writers."[2]

THE CHURCH'S ROLE IS TO PROVIDE AN ATMOSPHERE IN WHICH EACH INDIVIDUAL CAN LOVE AND BE LOVED IN INTIMATE RELATIONSHIPS WITH OTHERS

Family ministry has a double focus: to care for, support, empower, and nurture families in the church; and to bring people together as a body in a way that enables authentic, biblical community to take place. Some argue that churches must choose between these two emphases (and many churches do). As we have seen, however, the Bible recognizes the importance of both the nuclear family and the church community.

Maintaining an equal emphasis on both of these aspects, however, is a massive undertaking that cannot be handled by a single pastor or other specialist. A theology of family in the church must be acknowledged, pursued, and facilitated by the congregation at large.

CREATING A VISIONARY FOUNDATION
OF FAMILY MINISTRY

Following the development of a theology of family and family ministry in the church, the second step is to articulate a vision for the church that clearly expresses that theology. Creating a vision or purpose statement that theologically supports family ministry is the best way to accomplish this vital step.

A good vision statement answers the question, Why do we exist? The answer to that question forms the unique reason God has called the body into existence. It further provides a template with which to process every decision, discussion, and plan within the church. Some churches sense a call to reach out to the poor or to provide significant social services to a community. Others seek to reach out to disinterested or disenfranchised adults. Still others have gathered with a global missionary mindset. Occasionally a church may have multiple purposes; for example, a church may have a mission mindset and contemporary outreach to an upper-middle-class community. What's important is that the entire church is aligned with the vision, which sets the stage for building a bona fide community of faith.

Perhaps you already have a well-thought-out and clearly stated vision. If that vision was created carefully using theological guidelines, you may be able to move through this step quickly. However, if your church vision was created for pragmatic or socially strategic reasons, you probably need to come up with a new one or change it to reflect your theology.

To determine if your current vision statement supports family ministry, you might gather trusted leaders in the church, write the statement on a flip chart or white board, and pass around a summary of your theology of family and family ministry. First, discuss and agree upon the theological statement. After you are convinced that everyone understands and is in agreement with the theology of family and family ministry, revisit the vision statement. Ask the question, Is there any aspect or phrase in this statement that violates, challenges, or even ignores our theological statement? This will help you determine if you should keep the vision statement as is, or whether it needs revision.

The vision statement is critical to the process because it defines what you would like to and even *should* do in implementing new ministry ideas. On the flip side, a bad vision statement can lead a church in directions that it theologically and biblically may not want to go. I strongly encourage every church to be diligent in creating a vision statement that supports its theology of family and family ministry.

CREATING A PHILOSOPHICAL FOUNDATION OF FAMILY MINISTRY

The final step is to develop a philosophy of family ministry that

- enables a practical response to the theology of church and family,
- takes into account the vision of the church, and
- allows for the uniqueness and distinctiveness of the church to be nurtured and embraced.

By building your family ministry on these three foundations, you will create a tailored philosophy of family ministry that fits God's special calling for your church. This is a key step in deciding where to go with the information in this book. It is essential that your church allows its theology of church and family life to shape how it views programs, events, and ministries, thus creating a unique philosophy of family ministry. This uniqueness allows God to work in and through your congregation as an intimate community that's willing to make changes for God's sake and the gospel's.

References
1. Rodney Clapp, *Families at the Crossroads: Beyond Traditional and Modern Options* (Downers Grove, IL: InterVarsity Press, 1993), 68.
2. Charles M. Sell, *Family Ministry* (Grand Rapids, MI: Zondervan Publishing House, 1981, 1995), 79.

IMPLEMENTING FAMILY MINISTRY

CHAPTER THREE

ONCE THE NEED FOR A FAMILY-POWERED CHURCH is recognized, and pastoral staff and lay leadership commit to doing something about the need, practical questions begin to arise. What is the *downside* of creating and implementing such a ministry? What are the pitfalls to avoid? What should we be aware of as we begin to move in this direction? This book helps you address those and many other practical issues. This section offers practical suggestions for moving toward a family-powered church. These suggestions are followed by four questions every church must ask itself when beginning to seriously consider family ministry.

SUGGESTIONS FOR SUCCESSFUL IMPLEMENTATION

VIEW FAMILY MINISTRY AS ORGANIC, NOT PROGRAMMATIC

Programs usually look like this: Ask a question, then provide a quick solution. For example,

- Is there a need? Create a program.
- Is there a voice crying out for help? Offer a class.
- Are there people who want a camp? Plan it.

When we respond by simply making something available without considering the long-range effects of our decisions across the church spectrum, we lose our ability to create an environment of community health for the entire church. A knee-jerk reaction to people's needs may be fine for the short term but will do more damage than good in the end. Decisions must be strategically made, with various options weighed from a variety of angles; we must not simply run with the first solution that comes to mind.

BE FLEXIBLE WITH THE IMPLEMENTATION OF FAMILY MINISTRY

People often want you to establish one model or philosophical way of doing family ministry. Such limitations, however, could hinder what God wants to do in your midst. Be as flexible as possible in creating a family ministry that builds community. Your ministry solutions should have far more to do with your theology, vision, and philosophy than they do with preconceived notions of how such a ministry should look.

EXPECT TO INVEST TIME WHEN TRANSITIONING TO A FAMILY-POWERED CHURCH

Even with a committed pastoral staff and laity, the ideas in this book cannot be implemented overnight. Dismantling decades of fragmented programming, leading an entire congregation into seeing church less as a ministry smorgasbord and more as a family of intimately connected families, and asking people to put relationships above structural agendas is a daunting task. But the basis of this book is that family ministry is a *comprehensive overhaul of how we do church!* The following well-known story highlights the importance of keeping the end in mind.

> *Dismantling decades of fragmented programming, leading an entire congregation into seeing church less as a ministry smorgasbord and more as a family of intimately connected families, and asking people to put relationships above structural agendas is a daunting task.*

A man approached a laborer who was laying bricks and asked him, "What are you doing?" The laborer replied, "Can't you see I'm laying bricks?" The man then walked over to another bricklayer and asked, "What are you doing?" The second workman answered with pride, "I'm building a cathedral." Both laborers were laying bricks. The first laborer was focused on each individual brick; but the second laborer kept the goal, and therefore the final product, in mind.

Keeping the goal in mind is critical when moving toward becoming a family-powered church, but so is being patient enough to strategically and systematically bring a church along at a reasonable pace. When we move too quickly or jump too fast, we may do more harm than good.

I recently heard of one pastor of youth and family ministry who left her job feeling defeated. Actually, she was encouraged to leave. She had enthusiastically embraced the idea of turning her youth ministry into a "family-focused" youth ministry. In her enthusiasm, however, she discarded all age-segregated ministries in favor of youth and family activities and programs. Her vision for being more family-focused was lost in the furor over too swift, too widespread programmatic changes. It's not enough to change our *programs;* we are ultimately concerned about changing the way people perceive ministry. And bringing about a shift in thinking takes time—time for ideas to seep out into all areas of church leadership.

NOT EVERYONE WILL AGREE, BUT PRESS ON NONETHELESS

Given the fact that we need to change people's thinking about ministry, it's important to recognize that any change will have detractors. Rarely do we find 100 percent support for a new direction. Change is painful, at least to some. Leaders who are vocal about a change in vision or philosophy will experience some level of resistance based on others' *perception* of what the change will mean. It's important to remember, however, that not everyone is happy with the way things are now. But it's also important to remember that if 10 to 15 percent of church members are resistant to a change, change will not happen without great discord.

Consider the following ways to deal with negative reactions toward becoming a family-powered church:

- Give those who are struggling an opportunity to be heard.

- Invite those with strong feelings into the inner core (i.e., provide some committees to work on various aspects of the model).
- Convince people by letting them see the benefits of some small programmatic steps in this direction, rather than with pulpit bashing or direct verbal confrontation. (See Appendix A for suggested ways to "Start Small.")
- Make individual and corporate prayer a part of any changes made.

Applying these suggestions will not only help you avoid pitfalls, but will build positive momentum over the course of time. Notice that each of these suggestions asks you to exhibit patience and think holistically. What they don't ask you to do is overhaul your ministry tomorrow. The objective is long-term success. Keep that in mind as you implement change.

QUESTIONS EVERY CHURCH MUST ASK

Realizing that the system is broken is the first step in developing an alternative. The following questions will enable a church to be honest with its key people before moving forward to reshape the church for the future.

DOES THE SENIOR PASTOR TRULY WANT THE CHURCH TO FUNCTION AS AN INTIMATE, FAMILY-LIKE COMMUNITY?

Pastors often feel threatened by community. In a typical congregation where there is little or no community, the preacher preaches to individuals. He or she is only responsible for trying to connect the text to the real lives of individuals in the congregation (as if that wasn't

Realizing that the system is broken is the first step in developing an alternative.

enough!). It's a far different matter to minister the Word to a church that is proactively becoming a vital, living organism and is functioning as a genuine family. In a family-powered church, the senior pastor cannot just deliver sermons to a scattered, fragmented group of adults; instead he or she must get to know the congregation as a whole, of which the pastor is a part. To be faithful to the idea of becoming a family-powered church, the senior pastor must be ready, willing, and able to allow the theology of church and family life to change every area of pastoral ministry.

ARE STAFF MEMBERS WILLING TO COMPROMISE THE VITALITY AND RESOURCES OF THEIR OWN MINISTRY AREAS TO BUILD THE ENTIRE BODY INTO AN INTIMATE COMMUNITY?

At all levels in the church, programs and personnel turf are major issues. One associate pastor may give a thumbs up to the entire plan—the theology, the new vision statement, and the unique philosophy of ministry. However, once his or her event is called into question or he or she is asked to combine training time with another department, the truth and depth of the commitment will come to light. Even small, single-staff churches need to ask this question as they almost always have lay people in significant leadership positions and these same issues will arise.

Individuals on the staff and in lay leadership positions must be more committed to the body at large than they are to their own areas of ministry. This means that programs, ministries, and church leaders must compromise with resources, schedules, personnel, and even job duties to make this happen. Philippians 2:1-4 speaks to this idea of selflessness:

"If you have any encouragement from being united with Christ, if any comfort from his love, if any fellowship with the Spirit, if any tenderness and compassion, then make my joy complete by being like-minded, having the same love, being one in spirit and purpose. Do nothing out of selfish ambition or vain conceit, but in humility consider others better than yourselves. Each of you should look not only to your own interests, but also to the interests of others."

DO THE MEN AND WOMEN WHO ARE INVOLVED IN LAY LEADERSHIP IN THE CHURCH BELIEVE THAT THEY FUNCTION AS A COMMUNITY WITH THE STAFF? DO THEY WANT TO?

Many times staff members are the only people who are asked to discuss and then eventually implement an emphasis like family ministry. Laity are often left out, and are told afterward what was decided, or are brought in too late to give their input. For a family-powered church to be successful, the laity must feel as included in the process and discussions as any member of the staff. A wise staff will encourage and allow the laity, especially those in leadership roles, to enter deeply into the process of creating a church where community is at the core and relationships are more important than programs.

IS THE LEADERSHIP OF THE CHURCH, BOTH STAFF AND LAITY, COMMITTED TO CONSISTENTLY LOVING, CARING FOR, AND PROTECTING EACH MEMBER OF THE CONGREGATION?

A custodian or children's ministry intern must have as much intrinsic value as the senior pastor. Likewise, a harried and lonely divorced mother of three is no less valuable or worthy of time and energy than the businessperson who seems to have it all. Once any person enters the church family, he or she must be afforded the grace, care, and focus that every other member enjoys.

Carefully considering these four questions will allow a church to anticipate what it must do to implement a family ministry. The questions are intended to encourage dialogue among the key players in the strategic movement toward becoming a family-powered church.

For the church leaders of the future, family ministry is not an option to be explored or a new program to be implemented, but rather a theological truth to be expressed through a new way of thinking. Or maybe it's an old way of thinking. The premise of this book is that, after all the models and strategies of how to do church, Scripture continues to speak loud and true. *We are called to be a family of families and to love each other as Jesus Christ has loved each of us.* There really is no other option.

"A new command I give you: Love one another. As I have loved you, so you must love one another. By this all men will know that you are my disciples, if you love one another" (John 13:34-35).

PART TWO:
RITUALS AND STORIES
ENRICH FAMILY MINISTRY

THE POWER OF STORY

C H A P T E R F O U R

"Children used to grow up in a home where parents told
most of the stories. Today, television tells most of the stories
to most of the people most of the time." [1]

—GEORGE GERBNER

MY FATHER IS ONE OF THE WORLD'S GREATEST STORYTELLERS.
When I was growing up, Papa would take every opportunity to launch
into one of his tales. As children, my brothers, sister, and I would often
groan when he began a new story. However, many of my fondest memories are of the stories he told and watching him tell them. In particular,
I remember the two-hour road trips to my grandparents' home and the
stories Papa told along the way. Mama would lead us in singing and Papa
would tell stories. Mama often told her own stories or added particular
details to Papa's. These trips were special times for my family and me.

Papa communicated the richness of our family history through his
stories as he vividly recounted his and Mama's many experiences. For
example, I learned that my parents met at a peanut boil at a neighbor's farm
at the end of harvest. The stories brought the experience to life—peanuts
boiling, the fire, the crisp evening air, the laughter of family and friends,
and the excitement of young love.

Just days after Papa returned home from World War II, he married
my young, beautiful Mama who was waiting for him. Papa told us how
nervous he was when he asked for her hand in marriage. I heard about
their simple, but beautiful, wedding—I still can envision Mama in her
navy blue suit as she tenderly said her vows. All this imagery came from
Papa's stories.

Many of the stories were humorous, like the one about Uncle Wib's penchant for moonshine. The family always knew he was making moonshine again when the pigs returned to the barn at the end of the day walking funny because they had gotten into the still. The humorous stories often led to opportunities to talk about the serious things in life, such as Uncle Wib's alcoholism.

I not only learned about my earthly heritage, but I also learned about my faith heritage through Papa's stories. He told stories, and still does, about the tough times, like the loss of my parents' second child at birth, and how God helped them through. Papa also shared stories about my grandfather's faith—how my grandfather entered into a relationship with Jesus after Mama and Papa were married, and how he later became a Baptist preacher. Through Papa's stories, a relationship with Jesus became real and something I wanted in my life.

> *The principle of a story can stay with us long after we have forgotten the details of the story.*

Cameron Lee, in his book *Beyond Family Values: A Call to Christian Virtue*, discusses the importance of narrative—the telling of stories—for families. The four principles he cites from Donald Polkinghorne are also important to churches, particularly those seeking to create a church community.[2]

STORYTELLING GIVES MEANING TO LIFE AND ACTIONS

Like me, you may have read Aesop's fables as a child or had them read to you. These stories communicated a very clear purpose or value. ("The moral of the story is…") Life's stories serve a similar purpose. Through stories, parents can teach children the why—the meaning—of our actions. The principle of a story can stay with us long after we have forgotten the details of the story.

STORIES REMIND US OF OUR PURPOSE IN LIFE

I was blessed to serve on staff at a church in North Carolina that has a rich heritage. During the Depression, this church had a particularly tough time financially. In an effort to raise money to keep the church going, many of the women of the church worked to piece together a quilt. Squares were purchased inexpensively by families and individuals in the church community. Their names were then stitched into the squares and added to the quilt. In the end, the church had raised enough money to help them get through the difficult times, and they had a physical reminder of the struggle they had faced.

More than sixty years later the quilt still reminds us of the people who sacrificed greatly for a church in a small, rural town. Senior adults in that church have told many stories of how their parents, older siblings, and families struggled to keep the church going and how God provided. They came together for the cause of Christ; they had a purpose. Through the stories, the church members are reminded that God has a purpose for each of us and that he is always faithful.

STORYTELLING PROVIDES A FRAMEWORK FOR UNDERSTANDING PAST EVENTS

*"We must always walk into the future
with an eye on the past."*[3]

The stories of the past and of our faith not only help us understand where we have come from, but they also give us tremendous insight into where we are today. The freedoms and achievements of African Americans in the latter part of the twentieth century, for example, cannot be understood or appreciated without knowing the stories of the past. Many of today's young people do not understand the importance or significance of the events of the 1960s for African Americans. They don't understand and they cannot celebrate *because* they do not remember.

Similarly, for many people in the U.S., Memorial Day is a time to celebrate the coming of summer rather than a time for remembering those who gave their lives in war. Thankfully movies such as *Saving Private Ryan* and books such as *The Greatest Generation* by Tom Brokaw tell the stories of those who sacrificed, fought, and died to protect succeeding generations.

Most important, a significant portion of Scripture is given to us in narrative form. As we read the stories of the people of faith in the Old and New Testaments, we gain an understanding of the history of our faith.

Telling the history and the stories of those who risked and, in some cases, lost their lives so that others might have a better life helps us understand our world more clearly. It further provides a lens through which we may view current events, giving us a view of the world that isn't limited to our own time and space.

STORIES MAKE US WONDER ABOUT LIFE AND ENCOURAGE US TO PLAN AND HOPE FOR THE FUTURE

As I listened to Papa's stories about meeting, courting, and marrying my mother, I was determined to have a husband like my father—someone whose eyes would twinkle and whose face would light up when he talked about our first meeting.

Even negative stories can offer positive encouragement to plan for a different kind of future. My mother-in-law Mary died from complications related to alcoholism, and my husband Rich sometimes shared stories of the personal cost of alcoholism in his family during his childhood. Rich told how he felt he had been robbed of his mom because of her alcoholism, and how Shane and Shari (our two children) had been robbed of a grandmother who loved them very much. Shari and Shane understood the seriousness of alcohol and drug abuse and made wise choices about drinking. I am convinced that their choices largely grew from the truths they learned from the stories about their grandmother.

THE PLACE OF STORY IN A FAMILY-POWERED CHURCH

Being a church family involves a commitment to telling the story from both an earthly and a spiritual standpoint. For the reasons cited, story is a key element in creating a family of families in the church.

Throughout Scripture, but particularly in the Old Testament, we are reminded to tell God's story as well as our own (see Deuteronomy 6:4-9; 11:18-21 and Psalms 22:30; 78:4). We can help strengthen families by teaching them the importance of telling their stories, stories both of personal experience and faith.

Additionally, storytelling has the effect of binding people together—an essential part of a family. As the teller recites the story, listeners are pulled into the experience. What's encouraging is that the storyteller does not have to be masterful for this connection to occur. Whether the stories are humorous, sad, or sentimental, the storyteller and the listener experience a shared journey that binds them together.

The connection through story is one reason people in our society, particularly young people, feel strong, intimate connections to celebrities. Television shows, news reports, and movies draw us in, and viewers often feel a sense of connectedness to the actors, political figures, or sports heroes in the stories. Think about the collective outpouring of grief over the deaths of Princess Diana and John F. Kennedy Jr. Granted these deaths were tragic; but

> *By emphasizing storytelling within the church, we can help build the kind of church family that will "rejoice with those who rejoice; mourn with those who mourn" (Romans 12:15).*

many people mourned these two individuals as if they had lost a family member, even though most people had never met them. That's the power that story holds. By emphasizing storytelling within the church, we can help build the kind of church family that will "rejoice with those who rejoice; mourn with those who mourn" (Romans 12:15).

HOW TO BEGIN TELLING STORIES

Church leaders can promote a sense of community by helping church members tell their stories. Here are ideas any church can use to begin building faith and community through story.

TEACH PARENTS HOW TO TELL THEIR STORIES

Storytelling is a lost art for many of today's adults. We are used to listening, not telling. As with children, modeling is the most effective way to teach adults the value of story. Encourage church leaders to provide opportunities for adults to practice telling their stories. Invite a fishing enthusiast to share his or her story with a children's Sunday school class when the class is discussing a biblical story about fishing (like the miraculous catch of fish in John 21:1-14). In adult Bible studies, allow time for instructive personal stories. Truths can be affirmed and relationships developed through these times.

Another way to teach the importance of storytelling is to offer a one-day workshop on the topic. Every church has at least one person who is an excellent storyteller. Enlist him or her to lead the workshop. Or, if that person feels uncomfortable with the teaching role, have someone else do the teaching portion of the workshop and ask the storyteller to give examples through story. You might want to enlist two or three storytellers. Promote the workshop as a churchwide event. Consider the four principles cited earlier, and allow storytellers to incorporate their own stories. Finish up by having a time when parents and other adults can share stories with the church's children and youth. Ask the adults questions to get their ideas flowing, and remind them that they do not have to be great storytellers. Here are some suggested questions:

- What do you want your children or others to know about you?
- What values do you want your children to learn? Think of experiences you had as a child or young adult that helped you learn these values.

- What were some of the most exciting experiences you had while growing up?
- Who were your friends as a child or a teen? What were some of the fun, sad, scary, or happy experiences you had together?
- What were some experiences through which you learned about God and his love for you?

TEACH CHILDREN THE STORIES OF SCRIPTURE

My husband came to know Jesus at the age of thirty-three. His family did not attend church during his childhood, so he had little understanding of the heroes of the faith. In his words, "My only frame of reference was Cecil B. DeMille's biblical epics. I thought Moses was Charlton Heston." Sadly, many adults today share a similar experience and have little knowledge of the great characters of Scripture. Teaching our children the stories of our faith lays the foundation on which to build solid biblical knowledge as children mature. I remember one pastor who was very structured in his delivery of sermons and relationships with others. But when he was asked to dress in authentic clothing and tell the story of Daniel in the lions' den to the fifth-grade class, he could give an incredible dramatic performance. Children who heard his stories never forgot them.

Not only do the stories provide biblical history, but they are also powerful teaching tools for children who are not yet able to grasp abstract thoughts. Stories communicate simple truths children can hold on to. Children may not be able to comprehend the sovereignty of God, but they can understand the story of the Israelites crossing the Red Sea and grasp the truth that God provides for his people.

TELL THE STORY OF JESUS

> The church is "to be the kind of community
> that tells and tells rightly the story of Jesus."[4]
>
> —STANLEY HAUERWAS

The stories we tell define what is valuable and significant to us and influence the kind of community that will develop. Self-help sermons, as well as topical sermons and Bible studies on issues of current interest and concern, are important for our emotional and spiritual growth. But Jesus should always be the central focus of our lives and our stories.

The biblical narrative is centered on the redeeming work of God through Jesus Christ. Through the narrative of Scripture, God's magnificent work unfolds for us with each page that we turn. Cameron Lee captures the narrative aspect of Scripture when he writes, "The church, of course, is that community formed by the story revealed to us in Scripture. It is a story that runs from creation through fall and covenant to incarnation, salvation and eventually the consummation of a kingdom that is already partially present in the believing church."[5] The church's emphasis on story must include a renewed passion for telling God's story of redeeming love in Jesus.

ENCOURAGE CHILDREN AND ADOLESCENTS TO TELL THEIR STORIES

My nephew has an incredible knack for telling detailed stories about almost anything. He can go on for what seems like hours telling the stories of the book he has just read or about what he did at school. In his excitement, sentences run together with "And, then…" as he progresses through the story. Many children have this natural gift of gab—a desire to share the events of their day with those around them. Often, instead of encouraging children to tell their stories, we discourage them because we are in a hurry or are too busy with the never-ending urgent details of life that demand our attention.

When we encourage children and adolescents to tell their stories, we communicate to them that they are important and their life

THE POWER OF STORY

experiences are valued. Furthermore, as children tell their stories, they gain the expertise to tell their stories as adults.

BE A "FAITHTELLER"

Whether your church is two years old or two hundred years old, it has its own heroes and heroines of the faith. Share with your congregation how God has brought you to where you are. It isn't healthy to live in the past, but remembering God's past faithfulness joins people together in a common vision of celebrating the past and hoping for the future.

Modeling is the best way to demonstrate the importance of storytelling. The senior pastor can do this from the pulpit, sharing stories of his or her family or stories from the life of the church (be sure to ask permission before sharing someone's story). Storytelling can also be included in teaching, newsletters, and church bulletins. However you choose to model storytelling, the important thing is to get people thinking in terms of story.

In Psalm 145:3-7, the psalmist suggests to us the long-range impact of the telling of our stories:

> Great is the Lord and most worthy of praise;
> his greatness no one can fathom.
> One generation *will commend your works to another;*
> they *will tell of your mighty acts.*
> They *will speak of the glorious splendor of your majesty,*
> and I will meditate on your wonderful works.
> They *will tell of the power of your awesome works,*
> and I will proclaim your great deeds.
> They will celebrate your abundant goodness
> and joyfully sing of your righteousness [emphasis added].

This is a psalm of exhortation, encouraging us to continue telling our stories of God's majesty, power, and goodness. The psalmist reminds us of the fruit of telling the story of God's presence:

As we tell, the hearers will meditate.
As we tell, the hearers will proclaim.
As we tell, the hearers will celebrate.

The family-powered church is all about getting families to meditate on, proclaim, and celebrate the goodness of God and the joy of being in his family. Story provides a fun and meaningful way to carry out these activities while at the same time building church and family traditions. There is great treasure to be mined in your church; story can help you uncover the riches!

References
1. George Gerbner quoted by Ted Schmidt in "The Breakdown of Community: A Catholic Response," GRAIL (vol. 9, issue 4, December 1993), 11.
2. Donald Polkinghorne quoted in Cameron Lee, *Beyond Family Values: A Call to Christian Virtue* (Downers Grove, IL: InterVarsity Press, 1998), 161.
3. Well-known legal maxim quoted in Phyllis D. Airhart and Margaret Lamberts Bendroth, editors, *Faith Traditions and the Family* (Louisville, KY: Westminster John Knox Press, 1996), 7.
4. Stanley Hauerwas quoted in Cameron Lee, *Beyond Family Values: A Call to Christian Virtue*, 178.
5. Cameron Lee, *Beyond Family Values: A Call to Christian Virtue*, 159.

THE SIGNIFICANCE
OF RITUAL

CHAPTER FIVE

RICH AND I WERE BLESSED TO LIVE CLOSE to our granddaughter, Cierra, until she was twenty months old. Most Saturdays Cierra would have a sleepover at "Nana" and "Papi's" house. (Nana and Papi are what Cierra called us.) The activities we did with Cierra on Saturday evenings varied, but every Sunday morning we had the same ritual. Breakfast always consisted of homemade banana pancakes with real maple syrup. Rich insisted that we didn't use a substitute—Cierra had to discover what real maple syrup was. Then after breakfast we would all go to church together. I'm not sure who was impacted the most by those Saturday sleepovers—Cierra, Rich, or I.

Rituals are the experiences that provide meaning to our lives. The favorite family meal, the particular vacation spot, the Thanksgiving feast at Grandma's house—all are rituals that enrich our lives. Rituals help bring purpose and vibrancy to life.

In every stage of life, rituals offer an anchor of stability in a chaotic, unstable world. For children, the world can be a frightening place. Rituals are something children can hold on to, something they can count on. Meg Cox, in *The Heart of a Family: Searching America for New Traditions That Fulfill Us*, reminds us what it must be like to be a child: "Think about what it means to be a small child…You never know when you wake up each day where you'll be taken, what you'll wear, which foods will be put before you. You haven't totally mastered the language yet, so you're not entirely sure if somebody, even somebody who loves you, will understand what you're hungry for or where you hurt. The world is vast, unpredictable, and beyond your control or comprehension."[1]

Children seek things that are predictable, things that make their world small enough to handle. Many children think of their own creative ways to bring a sense of safety to their worlds—including security blankets, night lights, and favorite stuffed animals (or pets). Rituals can provide that something for children to grab hold of.

Children are not the only ones who benefit from the power of rituals. Adults, in particular senior adults, can also face a scary world. When dealing with the frightening aspects of old age, including failing health and loss of friends and family, senior adults can find solace or security in rituals. For example, in the small town in North Carolina where I lived, a group of senior adult men met every weekday morning at a local fast food restaurant for breakfast. In a very real sense, that morning event was their "security blanket."

In every stage of life, rituals offer an anchor of stability in a chaotic, unstable world.

According to Meg Cox, rituals also have the power to comfort, heal, and teach.[2] The ritual of tucking a small child in at night and praying together provides comfort, makes the day's hurts better, and teaches the child that he or she is loved and that God cares. Simple rituals provide valuable experiences.

Like the simple act of saying good night to a child, rituals do not have to be grand, elaborate events or experiences, although they can be. The size or extravagance of the ritual is not what's important. When I was a child, one of my favorite experiences was to hurry home from church on Sunday night with my family to eat a supper of banana sandwiches while we watched *The Ed Sullivan Show* together. My husband Rich grew up in a family where dinner was a rather formal event every evening, except on Saturdays. On Saturdays, his mother fixed dinner and the family ate on TV trays in the family room and watched *Gunsmoke* together. Rich's grandfather usually walked from his house down the street to join them. Neither of these events required a great deal of planning and preparation, but they were important and memorable experiences.

With a little creativity, many ordinary, everyday events can become extraordinary. Parents might want to create rituals out of ordinary events such as

- saying good night to children,
- going to sports practice,
- eating meals together,
- visiting grandparents,
- watching a television program,
- watching a particular movie, or
- cleaning the bedroom (or doing other chores).

THE BASICS OF RITUAL

Simple changes can transform ordinary events into rituals. Here are five basic elements that must be present to raise an experience beyond the everyday experiences of life.

EXPERIENCE

The heart of ritual is experience, including both actions and words. Ritual involves the doing of something. Attending the Christmas Eve service, the annual July family reunion, or the husband-and-wife date night every Thursday all invite the participants to actively take part in the experience.

REPETITION

For an event to be considered a ritual, it must be something that regularly reoccurs, such as the annual family pilgrimage to the beach or tucking in your child every night. The repetitive nature of the event raises it beyond the ordinary.

Some ceremonial rituals, such as weddings or funerals, are one-time events; the repetition involves the way in which the events are celebrated or observed. For example, churches or families usually include particular elements in all weddings, even though each wedding is a one-time event and may be tailored for the families involved. The same holds true for funerals. Families and church communities often have specific ways of mourning the loss and celebrating the life of individuals who have died. Expectations of how a ceremonial event should or should not look run through these events, creating a similar repetitive effect on other types of rituals.

DRAMA AND SYMBOLISM

Meg Cox calls the dramatic element in a ritual a "focused, heightened mood."[3] Again, this element of ritual may be simple and subtle. For example, a friend of mine makes a ritual of brushing her teeth. Every evening she and her two boys gather in the bathroom in front of the mirror. The boys spread toothpaste on their toothbrushes, joining in with their mother to sing a little song about brushing teeth. There is an energy and excitement present that takes the toothbrushing experience to the level of ritual. Whether the mood is upbeat, sad, or celebratory, this elevated sense of emotion is a necessary element to move the ordinary to the extraordinary experience of ritual.

> *An elevated sense of emotion is a necessary element to move the ordinary to the extraordinary experience of ritual.*

The use of symbolism is also a necessary characteristic. The symbols of our major holiday rituals can be easily identified: food, fowl, and football at Thanksgiving; trees, presents, and the nativity at Christmas. Symbols in smaller, simpler rituals are important as well. For the annual trip to the beach it might be a favorite lawn chair, a favorite spot on the beach, or particular meals.

An easy way to identify the symbols in the rituals of your childhood is to think of the things that, when you see them, hear them, or even smell them, immediately take you back to a particular experience. The smell of Thanksgiving dinner always makes me think of my aunt's house where we spent every Thanksgiving when I was a child. Symbols help cement ritual events in our memories.

ORDER

Ritual does not require elaborate structure. There should be flexibility to allow for change or adaptation when needed. Even so, a set order, or "prescribed sequence of events," is a necessary component.[4]

Our family has had a particular Christmas ritual for almost twenty years. We still go through the same sequence of events even though our children are now adults. First, on Christmas Eve, each member of the family opens one gift just before we go to bed. This aspect of the ritual developed when our son was small and could hardly wait for Christmas morning. In an effort to calm him down enough to sleep, we allowed him to open one present. It's been a part of the ritual every since. We are not morning people, except for Christmas morning. Whoever gets up first starts the coffee and wakes up everybody else. As people get up and get dressed, we begin to prepare breakfast. We don't have a set Christmas breakfast, but we always eat breakfast first. After breakfast we gather around the tree and someone reads Luke 2. We talk about the true meaning of Christmas and then pray together.

Next, we choose someone to be Santa and that person takes down the stockings containing small, inexpensive gifts and cards we have brought for each other. We spend the next few minutes reading the cards (as our children have grown older the card exchange has taken on greater significance). Then we begin the process of opening the gifts. We go around the circle, and each person opens one gift at a time. We take a few minutes to comment on the significance of the gift, laugh about it, or model it. Sometimes we stop for a cup of hot chocolate or a snack and then return to opening gifts. The extravagance or cost of the present is not important; the goal is to celebrate the gift and the giver.

There is room for flexibility, and the ritual has been modified as

THE FAMILY-POWERED CHURCH

our children have grown older. However, the basic order has stayed the same through the years. On occasion someone has suggested a change, such as not opening one gift on Christmas Eve; but everyone else always vetoes it. We want to do what is familiar—the way we have always done it. (Have you heard that phrase before?) The continuity and the order underscore the importance of the experience.

COMMUNICATION OF TRUTHS

Because ritual experiences are extraordinary, they often communicate truths. Ritual teaches us what's important and valuable. My friend's toothbrushing ritual with her two boys teaches them the importance of dental hygiene. Family trips to the beach every year can teach several truths: (1) family time is important, (2) fun and relaxation are important for our emotional health, and (3) without sunscreen you will become sunburned. The structure and activities of each particular ritual determine the truths each family learns. It's important to note, however, that not all truths are accurate or healthy. Some families are locked in to a ritual of fighting and arguing during holiday times; the values communicated during such rituals are negative.

COLLECTIVE DIMENSION

A "collective dimension" is also an important element of ritual, as noted by Joan Laird.[5] The collective dimension comes into play when more than one person is involved in observing a particular ritual. Although some have argued that a collective dimension is an essential element of ritual, it is not always required. I have a friend who wakes every morning, puts on her bathrobe, fixes a pot of coffee and toast with orange marmalade, and goes out to her sun porch for a few minutes to greet the morning. She listens to the sounds of the

Rituals, in some sense, work to unite people in a common purpose.

neighborhood waking up and spends a few moments reading Scripture and praying. She does this every day.

My friend's morning ritual is more than just routine. It has all of the basic elements of ritual. The excitement with which she looks forward to her morning, the repetitive action, the order of events, the heightened sense of emotion, and even the symbolism of the different aspects of the ritual (coffee, bathrobe, and sun porch) all make her experience a personal ritual. If someone else joined her in this activity, it would take away from the experience and deprive her of the renewal she receives during this time.

For most of us, ritual is seldom experienced in solitary pursuits. It takes the collective dimension to elevate the moment and create the energy so vital to ritual.

For most of us, however, ritual is seldom experienced in solitary pursuits. It takes the collective dimension to elevate the moment and create the energy so vital to ritual.

This book presents an approach to family ministry based on the idea of a family of families, so it is essential to understand the importance of the collective dimension in ritual. The traditions of our faith such as baptism, confirmation, and the Lord's Supper are more fully experienced when celebrated as a community. Even elements of the worship service such as reading the Apostles' Creed and corporate reading of Scripture can become rituals, giving them greater power to impact the community. Rituals, in some sense, work to unite people in a common purpose: "It [ritual] contains a social message; it joins and connects people or inducts a person into a community of peers and thus is a very powerful force in developing and maintaining the continuity of a group. The sharing of...rituals in a faith community...strengthens the social network and creates a system that is not unlike a large extended family."[6]

Rituals, of both faith and family, strengthen the social network by giving a church community a strong sense of identity. Ritual brings people together as a group and says this is who we are, this is why we are, and this is how we are.

In our fast-paced, rapidly changing culture, ritual is a positive means of acknowledging and incorporating change in our lives. Through ritual, change can be experienced more profoundly and yet more simply and smoothly. For example, during the first major holiday after the loss of a loved one, rituals can help us navigate the loss even as we adapt the rituals to accommodate the changes. As we experience this holiday, each element of its tradition will sharpen our awareness of the loss, but at the same time provide a means for coping with and moving on after the loss. Even with positive changes that we celebrate, such as marriage and graduation, rituals provide a means for making the transition into new territory.

In our fast-paced, rapidly changing culture, ritual is a positive means of acknowledging and incorporating change in our lives.

As we collectively share ritual experiences, we are taught the values of our religious heritage as well as practical skills. As we regularly participate in the celebration of unison reading of Scripture, for example, we learn the process and we learn what the church values. Family rituals can teach us as well. Through my friend's toothbrushing ritual, her sons learned the proper way to brush their teeth.

In addition, through communal ritual experiences we find comfort and security. That's one reason we so often hear people say, "We've never done it that way before." The rituals have provided a sense of stability. That doesn't mean we never change the way we do things. Remember that ritual is a valuable tool to use when incorporating change into our lives. Make use of this knowledge. People will be more comfortable if you can find ways to restore or create a sense of ritual during times of change.

CREATING RITUAL FROM THE ORDINARY

Sadly, many of our churches have lost the power to impact through ritual. So much of what we do has become routine. We continue to do things the same old way with little enthusiasm and sense of excitement. As a result, the traditions of our faith have lost the power to impact. However, often it takes very little effort to reinvigorate old traditions and make them come alive again. For example, when his children were younger, my older brother and his family regularly drove two hours to visit my folks. Along the way, there was an old-fashioned ice cream store. Danny and his family stopped there both on the way to Mom's house and again on the way home, and it soon became a regular ritual. With a little bit of creativity, the ordinary, two-hour road trip became part of a ritual. With slight adjustments and maybe a little ingenuity, your traditions, too, can gain new life.

Recently I attended a seminary graduation where those in attendance sang the treasured hymn, "Great Is Thy Faithfulness." Many others and I read the program ahead of time and wondered why we couldn't sing something a bit more festive or more contemporary. Before we stood up to sing, the president of the seminary talked about some of the difficult things that many of us had faced during the previous year and reminded us of God's incredible goodness and faithfulness. He further reminded us that not only were we there that night to celebrate the achievements of those who had worked hard to complete an education, but we were also there to celebrate God's faithfulness in seeing them through. I have never heard that song sung with such power and enthusiasm. The mundane became extraordinary.

BRINGING OLD TRADITIONS TO LIFE

There are a few simple ways to take our traditions and raise them to the level of ritual. First take a moment to make a list of the valued traditions of your church—things such as baptism, confirmation, the Lord's Supper, Christmas Eve service, and Easter sunrise service. Then evaluate each one, asking the following questions:

- Why do we do _____ the way we do?
- What changes can we make in the process that would make it more meaningful?
- Does the church family know the meaning and significance of this tradition?
- How can we pass on the significance of this tradition to others?

In the small, inner-city church where we worshipped in Denver, adult baptism is a powerful ritual. Before each baptism, the pastor acknowledges the importance of the moment by reminding the congregation of the spiritual significance. Then he tells who will be baptized that morning, who will do the baptizing, and why. The people being baptized each select a family member or friend to baptize them—someone who had particular significance in their spiritual development. As the pastor tells the stories of the relationships between the people who are doing the baptizing and those being baptized, the experience becomes more intimate and personal. The congregation is drawn in and joins in the celebration. With some forethought and with some slight changes, baptism in that church has become a life-changing event.

Rituals can be powerful experiences, whether they are family rituals or church rituals. They don't guarantee the development of a strong, healthy Christian adult, nor do they ensure a strong, healthy family. Vibrant and enriching experiences of ritual do, however, provide an atmosphere that encourages families and churches to be strong and healthy, and they provide the emotional connections that are so essential to a family-powered church.

References
1. Meg Cox, *The Heart of a Family: Searching America for New Traditions That Fulfill Us* (New York, NY: Random House, 1998), 4-5.
2. Meg Cox, *The Heart of a Family: Searching America for New Traditions That Fulfill Us*, xi.
3. Meg Cox, *The Heart of a Family: Searching America for New Traditions That Fulfill Us*, 6.
4. Meg Cox, *The Heart of a Family: Searching America for New Traditions That Fulfill Us*, 6.
5. Joan Laird, "Using Church and Family Ritual," in *The Church's Ministry With Families*, edited by Diana S. Richmond Garland and Diane L. Pancoast (Dallas, TX: Word Publishing, 1990), 112.
6. Joan Laird, "Using Church and Family Ritual," in *The Church's Ministry With Families*, 112.

THE CELEBRATION OF RITES OF PASSAGE

CHAPTER SIX

IN MANY CULTURES, LIFE CHANGES such as puberty, marriage, and the birth of a first child are celebrated with great fanfare. In our contemporary American culture, however, we have lost the sense of passion and celebration for many of the transitions in our lives. With the loss of rites-of-passage rituals in our culture, adolescents have established their own rituals such as getting tattoos and body piercings.

Churches can help families identify transitions in their lives that they might celebrate in positive and meaningful ways. These markers do not necessarily have to be major accomplishments, nor do they need to be major, life-changing events. The following list includes some of the transitions that families can transform into rites-of-passage events:

- a child's graduation from kindergarten
- the loss of a child's first tooth
- the first sleepover
- the beginning of the school year
- getting a driver's license
- high school graduation

Encourage families to celebrate in wacky, weird, and wild ways. Meg Cox shares some of the more interesting rites of passages that families develop. One family celebrates when a child reaches the age of twelve by allowing the child to have his or her first cup of coffee. In another family, the children are allowed to give their father the haircut of their choice when they complete eighth grade.[1]

Churches can help families define what they might use as rites-of-passage rituals to smooth and to celebrate the transition from childhood to adulthood. Churches can also establish rites-of-passage rituals as a part of leadership development for children and adolescents. Rites of passage in a church context serve to further the transition from a believer who craves pure spiritual milk (1 Peter 2:2) to a believer who is fit for the solid food of the mature believer (Hebrews 5:14). Particularly important for adolescents, rites of passage prepare them for growing leadership in the church and develop a foundation that will last beyond the youth-group years.

Most youth workers with tenure have had the heartbreaking experience of watching a young adult walk away from church and their faith, even though the young person was an active, committed member of a youth group and church. Mark 4:2-6; 13-17 (the parable of the sower) seems to speak to this phenomenon:

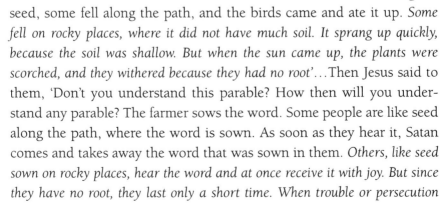

Rites of passage in a church context serve to further the transition from a believer who craves pure spiritual milk (1 Peter 2:2) to a believer who is fit for the solid food of the mature believer (Hebrews 5:14).

"[Jesus] taught them many things by parables, and in his teaching said: 'Listen! A farmer went out to sow his seed. As he was scattering the seed, some fell along the path, and the birds came and ate it up. *Some fell on rocky places, where it did not have much soil. It sprang up quickly, because the soil was shallow. But when the sun came up, the plants were scorched, and they withered because they had no root'*...Then Jesus said to them, 'Don't you understand this parable? How then will you understand any parable? The farmer sows the word. Some people are like seed along the path, where the word is sown. As soon as they hear it, Satan comes and takes away the word that was sown in them. *Others, like seed sown on rocky places, hear the word and at once receive it with joy. But since they have no root, they last only a short time. When trouble or persecution comes because of the word, they quickly fall away'"* [emphasis added].

The situation that Jesus describes seems to be what many adolescents experience. In their early teen years (or even younger), they enthusiastically embrace Jesus and the church. But as they enter their late teen years, graduate from high school, go off to college, and enter the working world, they face challenges to their faith that they aren't prepared to handle. As Jesus says, their faith is shallow, without root, and it cannot withstand the challenges of the world.

I recently visited a church where I served as youth pastor in the early '90s. I took the opportunity to catch up with some of the former members of my youth group. Many were now in college, some were married, and others were working.

Of course, I was interested to find out where these young adults were in their relationship with God. I was saddened and surprised by what I discovered. In some cases, the ones I had counted on to grow in their faith had walked away from the church. Others who had not been very active in youth group are now enthusiastic, young Christian leaders. As I pressed for answers to this phenomenon, it seemed that if young people had been given opportunities to develop their own gifts and leadership skills, this was a strong indicator of long-term faith development. For example, one young man had been somewhat active in youth group, but he was not at every Bible study and youth retreat. A crucial influence in his life seems to have been the opportunity to play in the worship band. Today he is serving with an international evangelistic music team.

ENCOURAGING RITES OF PASSAGE

As children and young people mature, it's critical that churches provide specific opportunities, or rites of passage, to help kids transition into strong, growing Christians. Rites of passage will vary depending on your church context, but there are a few universal principles. Gradually allowing young people to take on greater responsibility through specific rituals encourages a positive passage into adulthood.

RITES OF PASSAGE PROVIDE OPPORTUNITIES FOR YOUNG PEOPLE TO DEVELOP THEIR GIFTS AND TALENTS

Family-powered churches take responsibility for developing young people into leaders, not just entertaining them while the adults attend church. In his book *Developing Student Leaders*, Ray Johnston writes about this responsibility: "Most youth ministries [or church ministries] go in one of two directions—they either *entertain* students or they *equip* students. Each route leads to a different destination. The results are dramatic. When we major in *entertaining* students, we will most likely produce *spectators*. If we take on the challenge of *equipping* students for leadership, we will produce *servant leaders*"[2] [emphasis in original].

Allowing children and adolescents to experiment in different capacities within the church and family gives them a safe place to test out who they are and what they are capable of doing. Even if they fail, church and family provide a safety net, and failure can actually become a good experience through which they find out they are not gifted in a particular area or they receive encouragement to try something again.

RITES OF PASSAGE PROVIDE OPPORTUNITIES TO PUT CHILDREN AND ADOLESCENTS IN TOUCH WITH ADULTS

Children in our culture are more segregated and isolated from adults than ever before. According to the research of Search Institute, adolescents need healthy relationships with four to five adults to smooth the transition to adulthood.[3] Children and adolescents could be matched with one or two adults and take on greater responsibility. If your church sets up chairs for worship service each Sunday morning, why not team up a young person, maybe a ten- or eleven-year-old, with adults responsible for setting up chairs? This would be an ideal way to put young people in touch with adults and give them an area of responsibility. Rites of passage do not have to be elaborate, just intentional.

RITES OF PASSAGE GIVE OPPORTUNITIES FOR TEENS TO PUT THEIR FAITH INTO PRACTICE

"Having spent a career trying to understand and help young people, I am convinced that the one primary cause of the tragic self-destruction of so many of our youth is that they do not know the work and satisfaction of living for something larger than themselves…Without large goals, life is barren, life is a burden."[4]

Remember the parable of the sower? Children and adolescents need to have experiences that foster the development of a deep faith. Many have a faith without actions. Many adults struggle with understanding the connection between faith and works. James 2:17 tells us, however, that "faith by itself, if it is not accompanied by action, is dead." Without getting into a deep theological discussion, it is safe to say that our faith is shallow and without root if it is not connected to action. For many young people, action is the missing element.

Young people need experiences that demonstrate the value in their faith—a faith in which they find fulfillment and purpose that will further the transition to a maturing adult Christian. They need experiences that say they matter to the larger church community. If we provide experiences of increasing responsibility as young people grow older, we establish a natural progression of faith. The following are some ideas and examples of service opportunities:

- helping set up communion
- participating in a worship team (vocal or instrumental)
- greeting worshippers
- reading the Bible in worship services
- making announcements
- assisting Sunday school teachers with younger children
- working in the nursery
- working at vacation Bible school
- helping in the church office (making copies and preparing newsletters or bulletins)
- serving senior adults

These suggestions can be adapted for your children's ages, your denomination, and your specific church community. (A sample rites-of-passage program can be found in Appendix B.)

RITES-OF-PASSAGE OPPORTUNITIES PUT YOUNG PEOPLE IN TOUCH WITH JESUS

As James teaches, action is an essential component of a deep faith. Even so, actions are empty if they are not connected to a personal relationship with Jesus. Giving young people opportunities to express their faith as they mature through childhood and adolescence is not solely about doing, but about being. If we don't challenge young people to come face to face with Jesus, we are merely teaching them to be "good" people. Ultimately the goal of any opportunity we provide is to bring them face to face with Jesus Christ.

A few years ago, I had an incredible opportunity to go to Guatemala with a group of inner-city youths to help construct an orphanage for homeless girls. It was a challenging and humbling experience for us all. The young people learned many valuable lessons about life such as what poverty really is and their own potential to touch the lives of others. During a Bible study at the end of a long, hard day, one of the young men remarked, "I really liked the time we had to play with the young girls today. You know, it was like we could see Jesus in their faces." This is the ultimate purpose of all ritual, including rites of passage—getting young people to see Jesus in their lives and in the lives of others in profound and memorable ways.

References
1. Meg Cox, *The Heart of a Family: Searching America for New Traditions That Fulfill Us* (New York, NY: Random House, 1998), 257, 276.
2. Ray Johnston, *Developing Student Leaders: How to Motivate, Select, Train, and Empower Your Kids to Make a Difference* (Grand Rapids, MI: Zondervan Publishing House, 1992), 15.
3. Peter L. Benson, *All Kids Are Our Kids* (San Francisco, CA: Jossey-Bass, Inc., 1997), 36.
4. John A. Howard quoted in Ray Johnston, *Developing Student Leaders: How to Motivate, Select, Train, and Empower Your Kids to Make a Difference*, 16.

PART THREE:
CONNECTIONS ENABLE FAMILY MINISTRY

CONNECTING
FAMILY MEMBERS

C H A P T E R S E V E N

AS MENTIONED IN PREVIOUS CHAPTERS, the contemporary family is under tremendous assault. We can debate the reasons, but the fact remains that most of today's families lead incredibly stressful lives. Many families are so fragile that they are ready to crack under the slightest pressure. One more stressful event (Susie misses the school bus or Dad has a minor fender bender) could cause everything to collapse.

Unfortunately, churches too often add to the stresses of families. Instead of strengthening families, we could be weakening them by our subtle demands on their time and by encouraging them to attend every event we schedule. Instead of bringing families together, we could be pulling them apart. The worship hour on Sunday morning has become the most segregated hour of the week—not just racially segregated, but segregated according to families and age as well.

One goal of a family-powered church is to bring family members together. But merely scheduling events or programs that bring people together is not sufficient; there must be a purpose behind what we do. Let's look at some of the principles regarding the relationship between the church and the family. These principles should serve to guide you in the development of programs and events.

PRINCIPLES OF THE RELATIONSHIP
BETWEEN CHURCH AND FAMILY

PARENTS ARE THE MOST INFLUENTIAL PEOPLE IN A CHILD'S FAITH DEVELOPMENT

"Like a rubber band, young people may stretch away from their parents' values during their teenage years. But when they become adults, they will ordinarily return to the core values of their parents."[1]

> *Churches may spend thousands of dollars on programs for children and youth, and they may hire children's pastors and youth pastors; but, although those programs are essential and wise investments, parents have the greatest influence on a young person's faith development.*

Churches may spend thousands of dollars on programs for children and youth, and they may hire children's pastors and youth pastors; but, although those programs are essential and wise investments, parents have the greatest influence on a young person's faith development. Evangelism and discipleship are not solely the work of the church. Parents are a vital component—the most important component. We must shift from viewing the church as the *primary* faith-shaping agent to viewing the church as a *supporting* agent for the family in the evangelism and discipleship of children.

In this case, the church functions as a part of the family—offering training, support, and encouragement for parents and functioning in the relationship of brother, sister, elderly uncle or aunt, or surrogate father or mother when necessary. This means that part of the evangelism and discipleship of children and youth is the strengthening of parents, who in turn strengthen the entire family.

HEALTHY PARENTS PRODUCE HEALTHY CHILDREN

In families in which the husband and wife consider their relationship satisfying and fulfilling, children tend to be emotionally healthier. Studies show that children in these families are better adjusted, do better in school, and may be able to overcome societal factors, such as poverty, that might otherwise have devastating effects.[2] In single-parent families, parents can model healthy relationships with other adults. This, too, will serve to strengthen the family and have a positive impact on the children.

STRONG FAMILIES MEAN STRONG CHURCHES

As families become stronger and healthier, the church, in turn, becomes stronger and healthier. As families grow emotionally and spiritually, their health will spill over into the church body. Conversely, families that aren't growing emotionally and spiritually will spill their sickness into the church body.

These three principles demonstrate the value of getting parents involved in their children's faith development. The benefits of connecting family members are incalculable. That's why there is no more important activity than bringing families together.

CHOOSING ACTIVITIES TO STRENGTHEN FAMILY CONNECTIONS

In the remainder of this chapter you will find a number of events and activities to help you connect family members to one another. As you look for ways to add events and activities, take the time to evaluate what you are already doing. Ask the following questions about the programs and events currently in place:

- Is this program or event absolutely essential to the vision of the church?
- Does this program add unneeded stress to families?
- What is the purpose of this event?
- Can I adjust this program so that it better accomplishes the goals of the church's vision?

As you plan a new program or event, identify its purpose and goals. Complete the thoughts in the following sentences.

We are holding this event or developing this program to bring family members together for the following purpose:

We will accomplish this purpose by working in pursuit of the following goals:

1.
2.
3.

Becoming a family-powered church requires that church leaders are committed to continually asking the hard questions. Part of asking those questions involves evaluating ongoing programs and events and thinking through the process each time a new event is planned. Initially this may seem intimidating, but as you commit to the process and gain invaluable experience, you will find it becomes easier.

Some of the activities that follow are designed to take place at the church, while some are ideas that families can do at home. Others are designed to give parents particular skills so that they can be effective leaders in their own home. Still others are designed to strengthen parents in their personal growth.

PARENT ENRICHMENT

Noted child psychologist John K. Rosemond maintains that a strong, healthy marriage is vital to raising healthy children. He states, "In a two-parent family, the marriage *must* come first"[3] [emphasis in original]. This means that in a two-parent family, marriage must be held in the highest regard. It must be the most important relationship within the family.

In a single-parent home, Rosemond suggests the parent must establish strong boundaries to ensure that his or her spiritual and emotional needs are met before the child's in order for the parent to be able to sufficiently respond to the child. As he says, "You can't supply anyone else's 'warehouse' unless your own is fully stocked."[4]

Whether a family is two-parent, single-parent, or blended, parents need to replenish their warehouse—spiritually, emotionally, and physically. The church, as extended family, can help parents understand this need and provide tools and training where appropriate.

MARRIAGE RETREATS

A weekend retreat or even a single-day retreat provides a great opportunity for spiritual and emotional refreshment for married couples. In almost every community, you can find people such as therapists, counselors, and pastors who specialize in marriage and family issues. Take advantage of their expertise or use a wise, middle-aged or older couple from your church community. You might also utilize some of the national marriage seminars and videotape series that are available. Topics of interest for marriage enrichment include

Whether a family is two-parent, single-parent, or blended, parents need to replenish their "warehouse"—spiritually, emotionally, and physically. The church, as extended family, can help parents understand this need and provide tools and training where appropriate.

- communication skills,
- how to grow together spiritually,
- surviving as the "sandwich" generation, and
- understanding your spouse's personality.

Marriage retreats are especially memorable when they include elements of worship.

SINGLE-PARENT RETREATS

Similar to marriage retreats, single-parent retreats seek to strengthen single parents through training, along with emotional and spiritual renewal. Utilizing the skills of experts in the field of single parenting, plan a time away from children that particularly focuses on the issues of single parenting. Suggested topics include

- loneliness,

- grief and loss,
- how to handle issues related to dating,
- how a parent can take care of his or her needs first, and
- spiritual development.

When planning a single-parent retreat, you may want to schedule a one-day event because of child-care issues, or you may want to take along other adults to care for children at a location nearby. This would provide an opportunity to work with children on issues related to being the child of a single parent, such as divorce recovery and grief and loss. If the group dynamics allow, you may want to spend part of the time bringing parents and children together to work on specific issues.

MEN'S AND WOMEN'S BIBLE STUDIES

Small groups are the most effective way to bring people together and provide an atmosphere of intimacy and community. Including specific groups for fathers and mothers is a great way of creating a shared environment of trust. Fathers and mothers can grow spiritually and gain greater knowledge and wisdom in parenting by sharing and discussing their experiences of parenting. This is particularly helpful if groups include parents of children who are of the same age or parents of children who are close to the same age. For

> *Small groups are the most effective way to bring people together and provide an atmosphere of intimacy and community.*

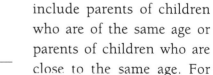

example, a group of fathers of teens could meet with fathers of young twenty-year-olds. Or a group of mothers of four- and five year-olds could meet with mothers of elementary-aged children.

PARENT SUPPORT GROUPS

Another way to strengthen parents is to provide opportunities for parents to gather around specific issues. All parents will experience a crisis, or a perceived crisis, at some time. Support groups can supply parents with the energy to cope with the crisis, resources to help overcome the crisis, and the encouragement of people who are walking a similar journey. These kinds of groups do not necessarily need to be led by trained counselors or by experts in a particular issue or concern. These are not counseling sessions. Parents who are familiar with an issue because they have lived it often make the best leaders of these groups. The list of support groups is almost endless. Take a look at your community to see what the specific needs are. Here are a few suggestions:

- mothers of preschoolers (MOPS)
- parents of teens
- drug and alcohol abuse groups (Alcoholics Anonymous, Narcotics Anonymous)
- drug and alcohol prevention groups
- divorced parents support groups
- divorce recovery support groups
- sandwich-generation support groups

One caution before beginning some of these groups: As mentioned in Chapter 1, people who need this kind of support may not feel comfortable approaching the church. The hard work of creating community and a safe place for parents to discuss the struggles in their families must be done before beginning many of these groups.

SMALL-GROUP BIBLE STUDIES

Depending on your particular church, small-group Bible studies that include parents and children meeting together could be offered once a month, once a quarter, or during the summer months. These times could include all ages of family members or could focus on certain ages (such as parents with teens or parents with preschoolers).

Many curriculum resources are designed for parents and children. (See the Recommended Resources in Appendix D.) The goal is not necessarily to revamp your entire teaching program, but to offer opportunities to bring

The goal [of small-group Bible studies] is not necessarily to revamp your entire teaching program, but to offer opportunities to bring parents and children together to study Scripture and to model for parents how they can teach their own children.

parents and children together to study Scripture and to model for parents how they can teach their own children.

Parents often feel uncomfortable or inadequate to instruct their children in spiritual matters. By providing a safe place where they receive guided instructions, you allow them to develop their skills and grow confident in this area. You can accomplish this, for example, by forming family groups and giving mothers and fathers instructions on how to pray with their children or talk with their children about specific faith issues. Help parents realize that teaching their children about God is not some mammoth task that requires a degree in theology; rather it is accomplished through small, simple ways of living out their faith in front of their children.

When I ask parents what they need help with, two areas are always at the top of the list: Parents want to know how to communicate with their children and how to teach their children about Jesus.

STUDY TOPICS FOR PARENTS

In addition to small-group Bible studies that *include* families, certain studies will help *strengthen* families. When I ask parents what they need help with, two areas are always at the top of the list: Parents want to know how to communicate with their children and how to teach their children about Jesus. Excellent resources are available to help you train parents in these two areas. Leaders in your church may also have expertise in these areas and could teach a four-week course. You could also provide information on other helpful topics including

- administering appropriate discipline
- relieving stress in children
- understanding today's youth culture
- strengthening parenting skills
- understanding the emotional, spiritual, and/or physical development of children
- keeping children from fighting
- teaching children to make friends

WORKSHOPS AND SEMINARS

Workshops and seminars can also provide useful training to parents. You might use videotapes, guest speakers, or leaders in your church to teach topics such as

- divorce recovery (for parents and/or children)
- violence issues
- drug and alcohol abuse
- sexuality
- understanding adolescence
- single-parent issues
- how to "blend" a family
- understanding today's youth culture

ACTIVITIES FOR PARENTS AND CHILDREN

These activities can be used as part of a family Bible study at church or as take-home activities to encourage families to spend time together.

MAGAZINE COLLAGE

Collect several magazines (each family will need about five). If you do this activity at the church, you might suggest that parents bring magazines from home. Have families each use pictures to create a collage explaining their family. The pictures could reflect favorite activities, dreams, their home, or anything that illustrates the family's identity and shows how each family is unique. Have families share their collages with other families. This is a fun way to encourage families to tell their stories.

TALK TIME

Churches cannot underestimate the importance of getting family members to talk with one another. In an article in Religious Education, John Forliti and Peter Benson write, "We found that the most important factor is parental modeling. Young adolescents who value religion are particularly likely to have parents who talk to their children about religious concepts, pointing out how faith makes a difference in their lives."[5] Bible studies are great places to get family members to talk. Encourage activities that generate conversations. (See the suggestions for Story-Time Month in Appendix B.)

> "We found that the most important factor is parental modeling. Young adolescents who value religion are particularly likely to have parents who talk to their children about religious concepts, pointing out how faith makes a difference in their lives."—John Forliti and Peter Benson

PRAYER TIME

Provide parents a topic for prayer and appropriate Scripture verses. For example, using Psalm 100 (following), direct parents to lead their children in identifying some of the things they can thank God for. Then have families close by praying together, thanking God for those things.

PSALM 100

Shout for joy to the Lord, all the earth.
Worship the Lord with gladness;

Come before him with joyful songs.
Know that the Lord is God.
It is he who made us, and we are his;
We are his people, the sheep of his pasture.
Enter his gates with thanksgiving and his courts with praise;
Give thanks to him and praise his name.
For the Lord is good and his love endures forever;
His faithfulness continues through all generations.

The prayer-time leader might say, "Read Psalm 100. Ask your children to name some of the things for which they're thankful to God. Help them identify people and things that God has used to bless your family. Talk about those things that are special (How does God bless you through your pet? What is it about Grandma that's special?). After a few minutes, close in prayer. Let each family member take turns thanking God."

INTERACTIVE CONFIRMATION CLASSES

For churches that have confirmation classes, the classes are an excellent time to bring family members together. These times can serve as refresher courses for adults and impress upon children the importance of this time because of their parents' involvement. You can include parents in the classes as instructors or participants or give young people take-home activities that would include parents.

FAMILY NIGHTS

Encourage families to set aside one night a week for family time. Family night could (and probably should) include having a meal together and participating in a planned activity. Many families seldom eat meals together sitting around a table. One psychologist estimates that even when families do sit down together to eat, meals usually last only fifteen to twenty minutes.[6] Mealtime can be one of the most formative times for children—a time with no outside interruptions and no television.

Mealtime is a great opportunity for conversation. I once heard a story about a man who grew up to win a Nobel Prize in physics. He

Mealtime can be one of the most formative times for children—a time with no outside interruptions and no television.

attributed his achievements to the fact that every night he and his family ate dinner together and had family discussions. He could count on his mother asking him, "What questions did you ask in school today?" He knew that he would have to answer that question at the end of the day, and it created in him a passion for learning.

In addition to eating a meal together, family nights should include a planned activity. These activities could include playing a board game together, playing a family game of softball or Frisbee, or going to the park or to a movie. To create interest in family night, parents should include children in the planning process. Depending on the age of the child, he or she could select (or cook) the meal for that night or choose the activity. Even small children can give their input on what they would like to eat or what activity they would like the family to do. Encouraging kids to be a part of the planning gives them ownership and creates excitement and anticipation.

FAMILY FUN DAYS

Family fun days are similar to family nights; in this case, families set aside the majority of a day together for a fun activity.

FAMILY NEWSLETTER OR BULLETIN INSERT

Consider sending out a quarterly newsletter to parents or putting a quarterly insert in the Sunday bulletin. (Enlist a family to publish the newsletter together.) The following ideas might be included in a newsletter or bulletin insert:

- simple, creative activities for families to do together
- ideas for devotions or Bible verses for families to read together

- parenting ideas for families
- articles or books families might want to read
- short notes from a parent offering encouragement or sharing wisdom gained from a particular experience

"SLASH EVENTS"

Events that encourage a one-on-one relationship between a parent and a child have often been referred to as "slash events" because of the names given to such events: father/daughter banquet or mother/son cookout, for example. These events can be tremendous opportunities to foster parental involvement with each child. There are any number of activities you might use including camping, fishing, hiking, or biking trips; movie nights; or mission activities. Be sure to include children of single-parent, stepparent, and blended families in these events. You might enlist singles or seniors to fill in as a substitute for a parent when needed.

FAMILY DEVOTION TIMES

Parents are often overwhelmed by feelings of inadequacy in this area and have many questions such as, "How do I do a family devotion?" or "Do I know enough to be the spiritual leader in my family?" Church leaders can help parents understand that family devotions don't have to be rigid, structured experiences. The goal is to get parents talking about their faith, telling what God is doing in their lives, reading Scripture, helping their children become familiar with Scripture, and teaching children how to pray.

Family devotions don't have to be complicated or boring either. In fact, they should be fun. God is a God to be praised and glorified—that's definitely not boring!

One simple way that a church I formerly attended encouraged family devotion time was by putting the Scripture verses from the children's Sunday school classes in the bulletin each Sunday. They also included a few questions that parents might ask to get a discussion

Church leaders can help parents understand that family devotions don't have to be rigid, structured experiences. The goal is to get parents talking about their faith, telling what God is doing in their lives, reading Scripture, helping their children become familiar with Scripture, and teaching children how to pray.

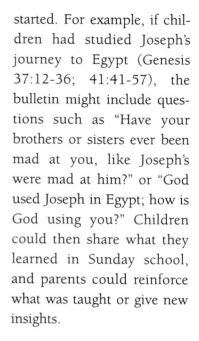

started. For example, if children had studied Joseph's journey to Egypt (Genesis 37:12-36; 41:41-57), the bulletin might include questions such as "Have your brothers or sisters ever been mad at you, like Joseph's were mad at him?" or "God used Joseph in Egypt; how is God using you?" Children could then share what they learned in Sunday school, and parents could reinforce what was taught or give new insights.

As you select which activities to use, remember to tailor them to the families in your church. Maybe there's a special feature you could add to one of the activities to make it more meaningful to your church members. Or maybe this chapter has helped you think of your own unique activities. That's great! What's most important is the end result of connecting family members to one another.

References

1. Mark DeVries, *Family-Based Youth Ministry: Reaching the Been-There, Done-That Generation* (Downers Grove, IL: InterVarsity Press, 1994), 65.

2. Mark DeVries, *Family-Based Youth Ministry: Reaching the Been-There, Done-That Generation,* 109.

3. John K. Rosemond, *John Rosemond's Six Point Plan for Raising Happy, Healthy Children* (Kansas City, MO: Andrews and McMeel, 1989), 7.

4. John K. Rosemond, *John Rosemond's Six-Point Plan for Raising Happy, Healthy Children,* 23.

5. John E. Forliti and Peter L. Benson, "Young Adolescents: A National Study," Religious Education (vol. 81, no. 2, spring 1986), 224.

6. Mike Lewis cited in Meg Cox, *The Heart of a Family: Searching America for New Traditions That Fulfill Us* (New York, NY: Random House, 1998), 10.

CONNECTING FAMILIES TO FAMILIES

CHAPTER EIGHT

FAMILIES TODAY ARE INCREASINGLY ISOLATED from familial relationships and from close social networks at a time when these connections are critically needed. Mary Pipher, a noted family psychologist, cites statistics suggesting that 72 percent of families do not even know their neighbors.[1] Suburban neighborhoods provide the option of retreating from the outside world. In fact, in many neighborhoods it is not merely an option, but a consequence of neighborhood design. Neighborhoods are designed for automobile traffic; people come home, park their cars in the garage, and close the door on the outside world. If people do go outside, they most likely take refuge in their back yards where privacy is protected by six-foot privacy fences. To connect with their neighbors, families must be very intentional. This dynamic only serves to heighten the isolation of the average family.

A family-powered church will attempt to restore connections between families. These social networks have the potential to strengthen families in at least two ways:

Mutual support. Families benefit from the mutual support offered by family-to-family connections. Runners often remark how the cheers of the people along a race route can give them a second wind and the strength to complete the race. Often the runners find stores of energy and endurance they didn't know they had. Families experiencing similar situations in life can provide this kind of encouragement and mutual support as well.

Problem solving and skill development. There are hundreds, if not thousands, of books on parenting. Most of us, however, are

THE FAMILY-POWERED CHURCH

> *There are hundreds, if not thousands, of books on parenting. Most of us, however, are ill-equipped—or at least feel ill-equipped—for the task of parenting. Family-to-family connections can help us solve the problems that we face as parents.*

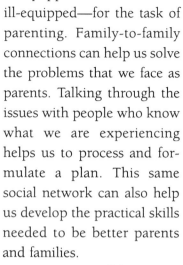

ill-equipped—or at least feel ill-equipped—for the task of parenting. Family-to-family connections can help us solve the problems that we face as parents. Talking through the issues with people who know what we are experiencing helps us to process and formulate a plan. This same social network can also help us develop the practical skills needed to be better parents and families.

The remainder of this chapter offers suggestions of how your church can plan programs and events that will help to make those connections between families. But be cautious about overhauling your entire church ministry. Take a look at what you are already doing and see if there are ways to make minor changes that will improve family-to-family connections.

IDEAS FOR CONNECTING FAMILIES TO FAMILIES

FAMILY-NIGHT SUPPERS

Many churches have midweek suppers as a way to encourage families to attend midweek programs. Often, though, people end up sitting at age-segregated tables. This is not always a negative experience since it's good to foster friendships among people of the same age. However, this kind of event is also a great way to connect families. As families come in, encourage them to sit together at tables with other families. Provide notecards at each table with questions for families to ask other families: "Where do you live?" "What school do your children attend?" "What is your favorite family activity?" and "What is the funniest thing that has ever happened to your family?" These kinds of questions can get people talking.

PROGRESSIVE DINNERS

In a progressive dinner, people eat each course of a meal (appetizer, salad, main course, or dessert) at a different location. Arrange to have families travel to other families' homes, fast-food restaurants, or even to a park for an outdoor meal. Be sure to include single parents, single adults, and families without children in your planning.

MULTIFAMILY VACATIONS

There are several ways to encourage families to go on vacation together.

- Enlist one family to put together a family camp event to take place over a weekend or for several days. Promote the event to other families. You could begin by setting a certain age limit for children (for example, parents with teens), or you could invite families with children of all ages.
- Center the vacation around a particular activity, such as white-water rafting. Plan it for a three-day weekend.
- Model family vacation times by encouraging staff and their families to get away together for two or three days. But remember, this is vacation time, not work time.
- Post fliers about various Christian vacations such as wilderness camps or cruises and encourage families to take part.

FAMILY BIBLE STUDIES

A Bible study group could be composed of two or three families who meet weekly. You might have three or four of these groups in your church. Or, if your church is large enough and committed to the concept of a family-powered church, it might be a full-fledged program in which many family groups from your church meet in people's homes.

REGULAR FAMILY EVENTS CENTERED AROUND A SPECIFIC ACTIVITY

For almost thirty years, friends of ours in Toronto have been meeting with the same Sunday school class around the game of curling. David and Barbara are now retired, but they began meeting with a group of young couples soon after they were married. All of these young people enjoyed curling.

The group is arranged around a semiformal association of other groups (church and nonchurch) who also curl. The teams meet once or twice a week for practice and for games during the winter. The season begins with a kickoff dinner at which everybody gets together for fellowship. The teams finish up the season with another fellowship and the presentation of a trophy to the couple who wins the season.

Groups in your church could join together around other activities or other sports such as tennis, softball, or baseball. The emphasis is not on developing a league or on winning. The emphasis is on forming community and enjoying one another's company.

Over the years the group has changed. Some members have moved away, some have died, and new people have joined. The group now represents a variety of ages from the late forties to the early seventies.

Groups in your church could join together around other activities or around other sports such as tennis, softball, or baseball. The emphasis is not on developing a league or on winning. The emphasis is on forming community and enjoying one another's company.

FAMILY WORSHIP EVENTS

Depending on your church, family worship events could be scheduled on Sunday morning, Sunday evening, or any other night of the week. Keep in mind, though, that families may be hesitant to spend one more evening out each week. You may want to incorporate activities into ongoing events. Consider having families serve as a worship team or in various other capacities of worship leadership. Plan music and other aspects of the worship service that will appeal to parents, children, and youth. If it's appropriate, plan to have a potluck after the service.

FAMILY MISSION TRIPS

Mission trips can be long weekends or weeklong events that bring families together to work on local or out-of-town projects. For example, if your church is near a camp or retreat center, you might offer your services for small maintenance projects. Many camps will provide food and lodging for free or for nominal sums in exchange for work your church members perform.

Family mission trips could also be arranged for national or international mission sites, such as Indian reservations, inner-city areas, or rural areas. There are many mission agencies that can assist in planning these kinds of trips.

ONE-DAY SERVICE PROJECTS

Like family mission trips, these projects are centered around a service activity; families join together to serve in a local ministry. Some of the possibilities are

- Habitat for Humanity
- food banks
- inner-city missions
- day camps
- tutoring agencies
- prison ministries

Check with your local denominational offices or local social service agencies for ideas of how families can join together in service to the needy in your community.

NEIGHBORHOOD FAMILY GROUPS

Many of our churches today are not neighborhood churches; people may drive many miles to attend church. It's not unusual for families from many different neighborhoods to attend the same church. Establishing neighborhood groups helps to restore a sense of community within the church by connecting families that live near each other. You might want to establish home Bible-study groups of families in a particular neighborhood; or families in a general area could get together for a meal on a regular basis.

AFTER-WORSHIP EVENTS

Many churches no longer have traditional "dinner on the grounds" events.

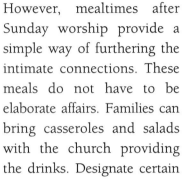

Establishing neighborhood groups helps to restore a sense of community within the church by connecting families that live near each other.

However, mealtimes after Sunday worship provide a simple way of furthering the intimate connections. These meals do not have to be elaborate affairs. Families can bring casseroles and salads with the church providing the drinks. Designate certain families to be responsible for setup and cleanup. Keep it simple.

TEAM-BUILDING RETREATS

We often think of team-building retreats as events for teens and young adults. These events are also a great way to build a sense of team unity within families and among families. Team-building retreats could be planned for a Saturday or a long weekend. Team-building activities could include segregated times for specific ages, but also times in which families come together.

FAMILY RENEWAL MONTH

This event takes a bit more planning but can be well worth the effort (you probably want to plan this at least six months to a year in advance). Choose a month as "family renewal month." The goal is to set aside time so that families are the focus of all of the church's activities. For example, each Sunday sermon during that month would focus on a topic of interest to families. Throughout the month, schedule special activities for individual families as well as events that bring families together.

Consider hosting a weekend workshop covering an educational topic of interest for families. In Appendix B, you will find an example of one church's family renewal month called home improvement month.

As you implement these ideas or create your own, keep in mind the goal of connecting families to families. Make sure that the activities you plan are simple enough for significant connections to occur. Try not to allow intricate details and expensive, time-consuming programs to eclipse the connections. Stay focused and you're sure to see results.

References
1. Mary Pipher, *The Shelter of Each Other: Rebuilding Our Families* (New York, NY: Ballantine Books, 1997), 84.

CONNECTING
THE GENERATIONS

CHAPTER NINE

*"Margaret Mead has said, 'The continuity of all
cultures depends on the living presence of at least three
generations.' One needs to learn how to be a child, a
parent, and an elder in a particular cultural context."[1]*

*"I have been reminded of your sincere faith, which first
lived in your grandmother Lois and in your mother Eunice
and, I am persuaded, now lives in you also"*
(2 Timothy 1:5).

WHEN SHANE AND SHARI WERE CHILDREN, they spent three to
four weeks every summer at my parents' home in north Florida. Rich
and I were always excited about our time alone. After a few days,
though, we missed the children desperately.

One summer, when our kids were eight and nine, we decided not
to take Shane and Shari to Florida because we didn't want to be away
from them for such a long time. One of the senior ladies in our church
counseled us to continue allowing the children to have that time with
their grandparents. She said, "These are some of the most formative years
of their lives. They need to have those times with their grandparents.
Grandparents can have a special bond with children—they love them
without any expectations. I think children learn what God's love is like
from grandmothers and grandfathers." Fortunately we listened to her
advice and, until they were in high school, Shari and Shane continued to
visit my folks.

Shane and Shari were also blessed to have had many close friendships with adults, particularly senior adults, when they were growing up. Interestingly, the children each formed relationships with older adult males who shared their birthdays. Shane and his friend Jim shared a passion for drawing (especially cartoon figures) and a keen sense of humor. They enjoyed playing practical jokes on each other and on other friends. Jim always remembered important occasions by sending a comical homemade card, usually accompanied by a cartoon or joke.

Intergenerational connections are important for adults as well as for children and youth. Sadly, however, the family and community dynamics in contemporary society do not easily provide opportunities for these kinds of relationships.

Shari and Herman shared a love of cats. Herman marked that connection by giving Shari a necklace with a cat charm. But Shari especially treasured the hellos and hugs she received from Herman at church each Sunday morning. These relationships with adults were extremely important to Shari and Shane; these friendships shaped and molded the adults they have become.

Relationships that reach across generations bring a richness and a depth to our character and have the power to positively influence our emotional and spiritual development. Intergenerational connections, like those between Shane and Jim and Shari and Herman, are important for adults as well as for children and youth. Sadly, however, the family and community dynamics in contemporary society do not easily provide opportunities for these kinds of relationships.

"We live in an increasingly age-segregated society. It is possible for a young student or worker to go for weeks without seeing a baby or an elderly person, much less being responsible for assisting them in any way."[2] Too many of us live lives that seldom intersect the lives of people from different generations. Many, if not most, of our social programs, organizations, and institutions are designed to serve or work with a specific age group for a specific length of time (preschools, elementary schools, retirement centers and retirement neighborhoods, Girl Scouts, and Boy Scouts). They do not have the purpose or ability to span the different stages of a person's life.

Mark DeVries states, "Apart from the family...the church may be the only lifelong nurturing structure left. Only the church and the family can provide Christian nurture from birth to old age and even death."[3] While the family does have this capacity, it has been diminished by demographic and societal changes. The church, though, has the capacity to nurture people at each stage of life plus connect the generations to one another.

THE IMPORTANCE OF INTERGENERATIONAL CONNECTIONS

There are four reasons that intergenerational connections are so vital to the health of the family and to the church.

INTERGENERATIONAL CONNECTIONS TEACH US HOW TO CARE FOR ONE ANOTHER

My younger brother Chris was born when I was eleven years old. Watching my mother take care of Chris provided many opportunities to learn how to take care of a baby. Not only did I learn by watching my mother, but I also learned through the experiences of changing Chris's diaper and fixing his bottle. When I first became a mother, I was much better prepared for the day-to-day demands of a baby than many of my friends were.

Similarly, when my husband Rich was nine, his maternal grandfather moved in with Rich and his family. Although Grampi had his own apartment within the family's home, he spent lots of time with Rich, telling stories about his years as a land surveyor and recalling the major events in his lifetime. Rich says that he "developed a great sense of history and the importance of history" from his grandfather. (See Chapter 4 for a discussion on the importance of story.) The time Rich spent with his grandfather also taught him how to care for and relate to senior adults.

Sadly, changes in the twentieth-century family have meant that many children do not automatically or easily experience the benefits of intergenerational connections. Families are smaller and children are closer together in age. Children don't often spend time taking care of a sibling who is much younger than they are or watching the "cool" older brother or sister experience adolescence. In the past ten to fifteen years, the need has increased for classes that teach baby sitters the basics of caring for small children. This is largely due to the lack of opportunities for young people to gain this experience in their own families.

Connecting the generations in the church provides an environment where each generation can learn the necessary skills to nurture and care for the others.

Further, people are living longer and healthier lives. As a result, many grandparents live very mobile and active lives and do not spend much time with their grandchildren, particularly during the children's formative years. Connecting the generations in the church provides an environment where each generation can learn the necessary skills to nurture and care for the others.

A church that seeks to bring all the generations together functions like a one-room schoolhouse. Staff and lay leaders of the church function as the teachers. In a one-room schoolhouse, older kids assist the teacher by helping to take care of and nurture the younger children. In this case, the "older kids" could be someone from any generation who assists the leadership in nurturing younger people. The "younger people" might be younger in the faith, or they may be people, young or old, who need to be nurtured and cared for.

INTERGENERATIONAL CONNECTIONS PROVIDE ROLE MODELS FOR CHILDREN AND YOUTH

Recently our granddaughter Cierra saw her first Fourth of July fireworks celebration. In describing Cierra's experience to Rich and me, Shari mentioned that after a particularly loud and brilliant explosion of fireworks Cierra exclaimed, "Oh, gosh!" Shari and I laughed and wondered where she had heard that phrase before. Over the next few days I began to realize how frequently throughout the day I said "Oh, gosh." Most of us have had similar experiences that remind us how powerfully we can influence others, particularly children and adolescents.

In our contemporary culture, many children and young people are influenced more by celebrities and peers than they are by adults outside of the family relationships. Yet adult relationships are so important. Most of the relationships young people have with adults outside of their families tend to be *influencing* relationships. Influencing

The relationships that have real power to influence our attitudes and behaviors, however, are life-changing relationships.

relationships do not have significant power to change the attitudes and behaviors of a person, *unless the person makes a conscious decision to change.* For example, I might like the way my friend Martha wears her hair or the way she treats her children, and I might decide that I want to be like her. I have made a conscious decision to change.

The relationships with real power to influence our attitudes and behaviors, however, are *life-changing* relationships. Relationships that are deep, intimate connections will result in changes in attitudes and behaviors that are *permanent.* We often don't even notice that the change has taken place unless someone remarks on it. The lack of life-changing adult relationships for adolescents is especially disturbing. Most, if not all of their life-changing relationships (outside of the family) are peer relationships. The church, though, can provide these life-changing relationships through intergenerational connections.

INTERGENERATIONAL CONNECTIONS TEACH US TO VALUE OLDER ADULTS

"Rise in the presence of the aged, show respect for the elderly and revere your God" (Leviticus 19:32).

In many cultures, older adults are regarded with great authority and respect. Contemporary American culture does not typically accord such respect to the elderly. Many older adults are relegated to nursing homes to live out their remaining years isolated and alone. Thankfully, this isn't the case for everyone. Even elderly people who are living vibrant and healthy lives, however, are often segregated from other generations, whether by choice or by circumstances. Consequently, we lose the value and richness that older adults can bring to our lives.

Connections to older adults provide us with a link to the past that can add richness and meaning to our lives. It further provides younger generations with wisdom gained through others' life experiences. "Is not wisdom found among the aged? Does not long life bring understanding?" (Job 12:12).

INTERGENERATIONAL CONNECTIONS ALLOW US TO PASS ON THE TRADITIONS OF FAITH AND FAMILY

Not only do older adults enrich our lives through the benefit of their wisdom, but they also are important in passing on traditions to succeeding generations. "Traditions and collective memories cannot be passed along solely through institutions such as schools [and] churches... Intergenerational contacts provide the opportunity to make them live."[4] These traditions and collective memories of family and church history function like glue, helping to draw the generations together with a sense of community.

> *Not only do older adults enrich our lives through the benefit of their wisdom, but they also are important in passing on traditions to succeeding generations.*

PROGRAMS AND ACTIVITIES
THAT CONNECT GENERATIONS

The remainder of this chapter offers suggestions for how your church can plan programs and events that will encourage intergenerational connections. As always, do some evaluation first before adding new programs or events. Many of your current programs, with a few changes, can be used to foster connections among generations.

ANNUAL "WILD OLYMPICS"

This is a churchwide event that includes the following elements (adjust these to fit your own church context):

- Use unusual Olympic-style events such as a three-legged race, relay races, or a frog jump (a variation on the long jump).
- Each event should be done in teams of at least two people.
- Teams are not segregated by age or gender. The goal is to mix generations, gender, and athletic ability.
- Focus on cooperation, not competition.
- Prizes or ribbons can be awarded, although awards do not necessarily have to be presented to the winners of each event. Choose wacky or crazy awards.
- Finish up with a barbecue or potluck meal.

TAKING CARE OF THE CHURCH

There are always repairs and maintenance that can be done on the church's facilities—use this as an opportunity to bring the generations together. Pair a senior adult with a young adult to paint a room, for example. Or organize intergenerational teams to do yardwork, such as raking leaves or weeding.

SENIOR-ADULT VOLUNTEERS

Encourage senior citizens to volunteer with younger generations, particularly youth and children:

- If your church has a preschool or day-care center, encourage senior adults to read to the children a couple of hours each week.
- Senior adults make excellent volunteers in youth ministry programs. They can work as ongoing adult leaders in direct ministry to teens or take on various short-term roles including volunteering as camp counselors or providing refreshments.
- Encourage senior adults to serve as tutors for elementary-age children.
- Senior adults also make great mentors for children and teens.

APPRENTICE TEAMS AT CHURCH

Not long ago in our history, a young person learned skills and trades through an apprenticeship to an experienced adult. Unfortunately, that's rarely the case in our society. However, the various practical needs of a church provide great opportunities to teach young people skills and make connections with adults.

> *The various practical needs of a church provide great opportunities to teach young people skills and make connections with adults.*

Apprentice teams could be set up with one adult and one teen or one adult and two to three teens. You might form teams to help with

- audiovisual and sound systems.
- computer systems. Many churches use PowerPoint or some other software to display music for worship, so a young person might help with the music each week. Or young adults might use desktop publishing software to help produce the church bulletin or newsletter.
- vacation Bible school. There are many tasks involved in planning and carrying out a vacation Bible school, including co-teaching, preparing and serving refreshments, helping to plan and set up games, and organizing supplies needed for

Bible study groups. Many of these tasks are great opportunities for young people to work with adults.
- teaching preschool and elementary-age children.
- tasks in the church's nursery.
- kitchen cleanup and setup.

RECREATIONAL MENTORING

Recreational mentoring teams are similar to apprentice teams. Adults work with from one to five kids to teach specific recreational skills. For example, adults might teach activities such as the following:
- fly-fishing
- running
- in-line skating
- skiing (water, downhill, or cross-country)

SKILL MENTORING

In skill mentoring, adults work with from one to five young people to teach specific life skills including

- changing the oil in a car,
- simple automotive mechanics,
- basic cooking or sewing skills, and
- basic computer skills. In this case, the young person might provide the training for the adult. Some of the topics covered could include how to use the Internet, how to set up a Web page, and how to use desktop publishing software.

CHURCH SPORTS TEAMS

The goal of these games is not competition, but cooperation. This does not mean teams cannot have fun winning. The emphasis, though, is on building community and having fun. Teams should include a mix of genders and ages (you may want to have a minimum age depending on the sport). If you have enough people for multiple teams, you may want to form a league, or you may want to set up an informal league with other church teams.

INTERGENERATIONAL SERVICE PROJECTS

Choose a short-term or long-term service project, such as volunteering with Habitat for Humanity, and put together teams with people of all ages. Encourage adults to teach young people how to do a particular task instead of doing it themselves.

ADOPT A GRANDPARENT/GRANDCHILD

In many families, grandchildren do not live near their grandparents; consider establishing a program in which older adults and children "adopt" each other to fill those particular roles. These relationships are almost always mutually beneficial. "Adoption" could include exchanging birthday cards or photos, telephoning each other once a week, and praying for each other. There are many variations on this program including

In many families, grandchildren do not live near their grandparents; consider establishing a program in which older adults and children "adopt" each other to fill those particular roles.

• a senior adopts a senior (a senior high school student adopts a senior adult or vice versa),
• a family adopts a college student,
• an older couple adopts a single mom, or
• a grandfather adopts a boy (without a father) in a single-parent home.

PRAYER PARTNERS

This idea is similar to the "adoption" programs, but may be a bit more comfortable for those who find it difficult to meet new people, especially people from other generations. People are paired up to pray for each other. Face-to-face contact isn't required, at least initially. Obviously, the goal is for a personal relationship to eventually develop. Take instant-print photos of individuals who will be prayer partners and attach the photos to 4x6 cards. On each card, write general information about the person such as name, age, birthdate, address, and phone number. Include specific prayer needs as well. The photo will help encourage a personal connection as the partners see each other at church. Prayer partners can be set up in any number of ways, including senior adult to child, kids in one Sunday school class to those in another Sunday school class, young married couple to senior adult, or empty-nest adult to a middle-school child.

CARE TEAMS

These intergenerational teams come together to meet with individuals and families in times of crisis. When a crisis occurs and the church staff is notified, the care team is called into action. The members of the care team provide many of the necessary practical items that families need but do not have time to think of during a crisis. Some of the items might include clothing, personal care items, pet food, and perhaps a large coffeepot (with coffee, creamer, and sugar), along with any other appropriate items. Care teams might also assist by staying with the individual or family and providing emotional and prayer support. You may want to have several teams in place that rotate throughout the year.

CREATING INTERGENERATIONAL WORSHIP EXPERIENCES

Many of our worship services include individuals from different generations. Seldom, however, do we consider how we might connect them through worship. Consequently, multiple generations may attend worship together but they are rarely *together*. Even if a church has separate children's worship, you might want to bring kids together with adults for a few minutes every Sunday or on special occasions. There are simple ways to encourage the generations to come together for an intergenerational worship experience:

Intentional fellowship time. Allow two to four minutes for the congregation to greet one another. Encourage people to reach out beyond their friends and others in the church they are comfortable with. Suggest that they greet someone from a different generation—someone who is not in their peer group. Be careful how you phrase your suggestions since some people in the congregation might be sensitive about their age. For example, avoid asking people to greet someone who is twenty years older (or younger) than they are. Encourage church leaders to be conscious of, and to reach out to, those in the congregation who might feel isolated or uncomfortable during this fellowship time.

Small-group prayer time. Bring the generations together for prayer. Depending on your church context, you may want to have people get into groups of four or five people for group prayer. Encourage groups to include children and youth. Perhaps you might give groups a specific topic to pray for, such as world hunger, a specific mission group, salvation of friends or family members, current community issues, or individuals or families within the church community. Allow plenty of time for the groups to get settled and to spend several minutes praying.

> *Multiple generations may attend worship together but they are rarely together.*

One-on-one prayer times for specific personal issues could take place after the service. In an inner-city church in Denver, four or five church members (adolescents to senior adults) come to the front at the end of each worship service. Anyone needing prayer can then come up for one-on-one prayer time. This period usually lasts five to ten minutes.

Visitor reception area. One church has a ten- to fifteen-minute greeting time after worship. Many of the staff are on hand to greet visitors, but church members from different generations are also part of "visitor teams" to welcome people who are new to the church community. One of the goals initially was to have children, adolescents, and adults available so that visitors of all ages would feel welcome. The result has been an intergenerational greeting for people who are new to the church community.

Intergenerational worship teams or choirs. Bring the generations together to lead worship. One way is to form regular worship teams composed of people of all ages, from teenagers to senior adults. Or you might periodically set up intergenerational worship teams for particular events. The result is twofold: the congregation sees generations working and serving together and the teams "share their hearts and life with each other through the power of music."[5]

Vary music styles. Many churches today have multiple services that reflect the worship styles of different generations. Even so, occasionally it is good to teach each generation the value and importance of other styles. Have someone share why a particular song has been important in his or her spiritual journey before the congregation sings.

CHURCHWIDE EASTER EGG HUNT

Set aside a Saturday close to Easter for a community gathering. Collect small items as symbols of Easter, and hide the items in plastic eggs. After your Easter egg hunt, ask church members (from different generations and families) to open the eggs and tell the story and significance of each symbol. Depending on your church size, you may want to have several groups of children and adults for the story time. End the gathering with a fellowship meal.

FALL COMMUNITY FESTIVAL

Churches often have an event for young children and families in place of Halloween. One church has a fall festival between Halloween and Thanksgiving. It brings together many of the positive traditions of Halloween (candy and costumes) along with a remembrance and celebration of the history of Thanksgiving and community traditions. The one-day festival includes the following elements, which you can modify to fit your particular church:

Old-fashioned Thanksgiving feast. Chickens and turkeys are roasted, smoked, and barbecued, sometimes over open pits. You can also serve traditional foods and foods with cultural or historical significance, including sweet potatoes, cornbread, popcorn, or venison stew.

Harvest booths. Various booths display and teach different aspects of preparing traditional foods or crafts. For example, one booth might have people churning butter and explaining to children how it's done. Other booths might include candle dipping, quilting, basket weaving, or portrait painting.

Outdoor games. Church members play traditional games, such as bobbing for apples, lawn bowling, and sack races, that might have been played at harvest festivals in the past.

I hope you now have a new awareness of the importance of connections in the church community. Without this awareness, implementing more activities will not help achieve the goal of building life-changing relationships; rather it will simply add more activities to the church calendar.

References

1. Diane L. Pancoast and Kathy A. Bobula, "Building Multigenerational Support Networks," in *The Church's Ministry With Families*, edited by Diana S. Richmond Garland and Diane L. Pancoast (Dallas, TX: Word Publishing, 1990), 177.
2. Diane L. Pancoast and Kathy A. Bobula, "Building Multigenerational Support Networks," in *The Church's Ministry With Families*, 173.
3. Mark DeVries, *Family-Based Youth Ministry: Reaching the Been-There, Done-That Generation* (Downers Grove, IL: InterVarsity Press, 1994), 116.
4. Diane L. Pancoast and Kathy A. Bobula, "Building Multigenerational Support Networks," in *The Church's Ministry With Families*, 177.
5. This is a quote by a senior pastor in one of our graduate student interviews.

FAMILY-POWERED
RESEARCH

CHAPTER TEN

AT THIS POINT, I HOPE YOU HAVE DECIDED that you want to move ahead toward becoming a family-powered church. But where do you begin? A good place to start is by looking at who your church is (i.e., who are the people currently in your church community?) and considering who you want to reach out to (i.e., who would you like to be a part of your church community?).

UNDERSTANDING YOUR CHURCH
AND THE SURROUNDING COMMUNITY

I recently worked with a church that was seeking to become more family-friendly in its ministry programs. The church was in a somewhat rural area and was near a university. The church leaders thought they had a good grasp of who made up their church community as well as the demographics of the surrounding neighborhoods. Because the church was a part of a major denomination, church leaders had the resources to complete a communitywide demographic study covering a five-mile radius around the church. The church also conducted an in-depth study of the people attending church and those participating in church programs.

Before the study, the church leaders had made the following assumptions regarding their church and the surrounding community:

• The primary attendees of church programs were older adults (empty nesters and senior adults).
• The surrounding community primarily consisted of blue-collar families with high school-aged or grown children, retired couples, and some young families.

What they discovered was very different. The demographic study gave these results:

• Families with small children (preschool and elementary-aged) made up the largest group of participants in church programs followed by college students and older adults.
• The surrounding community primarily consisted of young couples with or without children, young singles (mostly graduate students), and college students living in multiple-family dwellings.

We can learn three very valuable lessons from this church's experience. First, if a church has been at a particular location for an extended period of time (more than ten years), the community may change without the church fellowship realizing it. Changes had taken place in the neighborhoods around the church and, for the most part, church leaders were unaware of those changes. The church leaders were making assumptions based on past history. Second, as church leaders, we have our own particular circle of people with whom we interact, and we often make assumptions based on who we know. In this case, the majority of the church leaders were middle-aged and older adults. Consequently, their circle of relationships included people in that same age bracket. So they made assumptions based on the people they knew without understanding the people participating in many of the church's programs. Third, we need to be intentional about discovering who comes to our church's programs and, if we are interested in reaching the surrounding community, intentional in learning about the neighborhoods around the church.

This church had the resources to take advantage of an outside consulting firm that prepared a demographic study and compiled data from the church body. This was an excellent way to obtain reliable data. Less costly and less formal ways to gather data can also be used. One method is to obtain information from government agencies (including federal census data or information from city and state governments). Much of this data can be obtained over the Internet. This chapter offers ideas on ways to gather and organize the information and suggestions for using the information in becoming a family-powered church.

IDENTIFYING THE NEEDS OF PEOPLE IN THE CHURCH COMMUNITY

Not only is it sometimes difficult to identify the people who make up our congregation, but it is often difficult in the context of church to know what the most heartfelt needs of these individuals and families are. As noted previously, we often make certain assumptions based on our own experiences that are erroneous when applied to the larger community. The five obstacles discussed below often prevent us from identifying people's needs.

WE ONLY SEE WHAT PEOPLE WANT US TO SEE

It is a sad reality, but church is not always the safest place to reveal our problems. Church is where we put on our best clothes and our best face. People are very often afraid to share their frailties, fears, and problems; other church members appear to have everything under control, so why shouldn't we? The end result is that many of the deep-seated hurts and issues are shielded from the church community.

INDIVIDUALS AND FAMILIES ARE MULTIDIMENSIONAL

As a child, every person learns to function in a variety of contexts. We look differently and act differently with our closest friends than with a stranger in the supermarket. We look differently and act differently with our co-workers than with our supervisors. We look differently and act differently with our church family than in our own immediate family. As a result, it is difficult to truly understand the needs in a person's life unless we know him or her in a variety of contexts. It is a rare church where members have those kinds of connections.

THE ABILITY TO KNOW EVERYONE INTIMATELY IS LIMITED

Like the leadership of the church discussed in this chapter, we are limited to our own circle of personal interactions. It takes time and energy to get to know people on an intimate level. Most adults can maintain that kind of deep connection with only a handful of people at any one time. But it is through those close, intimate relationships that we begin to understand the true needs of an individual. Even in a mid-sized church of 250-500 members it is very difficult for the church leadership to have the kind of relationships necessary to identify the needs of the congregation.

WE MAKE ASSUMPTIONS BASED ON OUR OWN PERSONAL AND FAMILY NEEDS

It's natural for us to assume that if we are dealing with a particular issue at a certain stage of life or because of a certain family dynamic that everyone else in a similar context may be facing a similar problem. This is particularly true if we happen to know one or two other individuals or families with a similar issue. It's then easy to jump to the conclusion that everyone must be facing that problem. As a result, churches often plan programs and ministries based on the known needs of a few. The reality may be far different.

WE HAVE LIMITED CONTACT WITH THE COMMUNITY OUTSIDE THE CHURCH

For a variety of reasons, many churches and their members have little contact with people who are outside the church but who live near the church in the surrounding community. Limited interaction with non-Christians or with those outside our church fellowship prevents us from clearly understanding their needs.

WHAT GROUPS DO YOU WANT TO TARGET?

The limitations highlighted above must be considered when determining the people from whom you want to obtain information. Consider the following groups as you prepare to gather information.

Church members. Obviously church leaders need to gather information from their church members regarding family issues and needs. Depending on how your church maintains its membership, it may be difficult to secure information from some church members. As we know, church membership does not necessarily mean church attendance. If this is the case, the church leaders may have to decide whether it would be useful to seek information from members who are not regular attendees. Of course, one reason for their nonattendance may be the feeling that the church is not meeting their needs; talking with people to find out what their needs are may be a step in getting them involved again.

Regular attendees. If the church focuses strictly on church membership when gathering data, people who regularly attend but who are not members may be overlooked. This is often true for college students, graduate students, and young mobile professionals who may maintain a church membership elsewhere. It's important to consider gathering data from this group as well.

People outside the church. The needs of those within the church fellowship may be very different from the needs of individuals and families in the surrounding neighborhoods. Church leaders should consider gathering information from individuals and families around the church, particularly if they desire to build relationships and develop programs to reach people who are not currently a part of the fellowship.

Targeting specific age groups. Based on the goals of your church, you may want to gather information from specific age groups in order to plan ministries for them. For example, if you learned that a significant portion of the families in nearby neighborhoods had teenagers, you might want to focus on adolescents in your church and in the surrounding community, as well as on parents of teenagers.

Be sure to spend sufficient time determining the people from whom you will gather information. The information will establish the foundation for all of the work that follows. It is essential, therefore, that you gather enough data from the appropriate sources to help guide you in the process of creating a family-powered church.

METHODS OF GATHERING INFORMATION

Information can be gathered in a variety of ways. As we interact with others, we often have opportunities to hear what their greatest burdens are. But we can sometimes miss important information in our day-to-day interactions with people. There are several means of gathering information that, if used wisely, can be valuable tools: surveys or questionnaires, small-group forums, and interviews. By intentionally asking questions that get at the core needs for individuals and families, we begin to establish a strong foundation for a family-powered church.

ADMINISTERING QUESTIONNAIRES

In Appendix C you will find four examples of questionnaires that you can use to gather information depending on the target group and the type of information you wish to obtain. To ensure that you get the best results for your efforts, think through your survey distribution method beforehand. If you want to reach a large number of people with your questionnaire, one of the easiest ways is by bulk mail. However, there are a couple of issues to consider that may impact the value and quantity of responses you receive:

> • What groups will you mail the questionnaires to? (See the previous section, "What Groups Do You Want to Target?")
> • How will people return the completed questionnaires? There are several ways you can collect them. (1) Include a stamped envelope with each questionnaire. Even so, the number of forms returned will probably be very small. (2) Ask people to bring the completed questionnaires to the church. Again you will probably receive only a small number of completed forms. (3) Enlist church volunteers to pick up the completed surveys. This option requires you to recruit and train a volunteer team and involves a significant amount of time, especially if your church is mid-sized or larger.

If you want to obtain information from nonattendees, consider having church members personally ask family members or friends in their neighborhood to complete the questionnaires. People are more likely to provide open and honest feedback to people they know and trust.

Another option for distributing the forms is to target specific meetings (e.g., administrative meetings for church leadership, adult Bible study groups, etc.). Again there are some limitations to gathering information in this way. First, only the people who actually participate in those events will have the opportunity to complete the questionnaires. Second, you will miss many of the people who participate in the larger church community but who may not be involved in these small-group events.

Probably the best option for collecting data through a questionnaire is during weekend worship when you have the greatest number of people on hand and you can collect the information quickly: "Conducting the survey at this time allows you to

- get results from 60 to 80 percent of the congregation,
- gather information from fringe members who may not come to Bible classes or return a mailed survey,
- send the message to the church that you're serious about meeting their needs,
- devote an entire worship service to a family ministry theme,
- prepare and inform your church about the family ministry plan,
- give the same instructions during the administration of the survey, and
- build a sense of excitement for the ministry."[1]

With good planning, the questionnaire can be administered in fifteen to twenty minutes (depending on which one you use). You may want to schedule the survey for two different weekends to catch people you might have missed the previous time.

LEADING SMALL-GROUP FORUMS

Another way to collect information, which may be used independently or in conjunction with a survey, is through small-group forums. These groups allow people to discuss in greater detail their needs and their ideas about how the church can best become a family of families. Church leaders will need to do a bit of planning to ensure that the forums are effective and involve a broad range of families and individuals both inside and outside of the church. You may want to organize a group of people to coordinate this task. Here are some guidelines and suggestions:

- Schedule a variety of different times for these meetings that will be convenient to different people (parents with young children, working parents, etc.).
- You may want to host forums targeting different groups such as senior adults, singles, families with young children, or families with teenagers.
- Have specific questions designed to encourage discussion. (The questionnaires in Appendix C may give you ideas for questions.)
- Arrange for facilitators to lead the forums who will encourage people to voice their opinions and give everyone an opportunity to speak.
- Promote these meetings and enlist leaders to encourage participation from as many individuals and families as possible.

Conducting interviews

A third method of collecting data is through one-on-one interviews. These interviews may be used independently or in conjunction with surveys. One-on-one interviews (or meetings with individual families) allow for in-depth conversation and may provide an environment in which people feel more comfortable sharing their thoughts. Once again, church leaders will need to do some planning to ensure that the interviews are effective and include a broad range of families and individuals inside and outside of the church. It would be helpful to have a group of people to coordinate this task. Here are some guidelines and suggestions:

- Identify specific categories of families to conduct personal interviews with, including single-parent families, blended families, parents of teenagers, parents of small children, senior adults, singles, and young couples without children.
- Enlist and train a sufficient number of interviewers to contact the families.
- Develop a list of specific questions for the interviewer to ask. (The questionnaires in Appendix C may help you in developing your own list of questions.)
- Keep the interviews brief, no longer than one hour.

Interviews and forums may both be extremely helpful, but without careful planning they may not provide the information that you need. Planning time spent beforehand will be invaluable in determining the specific groups and families from which you wish to gather information so that you gain information from a broad spectrum. Otherwise you run the risk of getting a distorted image of the needs of your community.

CHARTING YOUR DIRECTION

Whether you use surveys, forums, one-on-one interviews, or a combination of the three, you will need to spend time sorting through and compiling the data you gather. As you wade through the sea of information, keep in mind the following ideas:

- Look for recurring themes (e.g., do issues of family communication show up repeatedly? or do parents have trouble talking to children about their faith?).
- Look for the strengths and positives of your fellowship. Identify the things that your church is doing well.
- Look for programs that, with a few minor modifications, would be more focused on the real needs of your community.

Once you have categorized the information, proceed slowly through the next four steps.

Celebrate your strengths. Take time to celebrate the ways your church is serving the needs in your community. Tell stories and share ritual observances that draw your fellowship together (see Chapters 4 and 5). Celebrate these strengths in worship and in other large gatherings.

Identify small steps. Identify one or two small steps to take in the next six months. Whether it's to have families participate in specific aspects of worship on a regular basis (reading Scripture, telling part of their story, etc.) or taking one regularly scheduled event and reshaping it to be more intergenerational, make the shift in minor and simple ways. Celebrate these changes and what they mean for your fellowship.

Do some long-term planning. During the first six months, pray over the information gathered and pray over the next steps. Prioritize the needs and begin to put together a three- to five-year plan for making changes to address the priorities. Share the information in formal and informal settings. This will keep the church informed of the process, allow the congregation to be a part of the changes, keep the enthusiasm going, and give church members an opportunity to bathe the process in prayer. Celebrate the small steps as well as the big steps.

Keep going. The process of evaluation and gathering information is ongoing. Consider doing brief surveys and interviews every twelve to eighteen months, particularly given our increasingly mobile society. Families change, families leave, new families move in. Extensive, in-depth surveys, forums, and interviews should probably be done every five years. Review Chapters 1 through 3 as you move through this process to remind you of some of the key principles in creating a family-powered church.

References
1. *Family Ministry Workshop* (Loveland, CO: Group Publishing, Inc., fall 1999), 13.

APPENDIX A:
ONE CHURCH'S STORY

I WOULD LIKE TO GIVE AN EXAMPLE drawn from a real church that has been moving toward becoming a family-powered church for the past several years. I will refer to the church as "Community Church." I don't offer this church's experience for you to replicate, but rather as a stimulus for you to begin thinking about how your church might become a family-powered church. This example could help you plan a course of action for your own church.

THE BEGINNINGS

A group of mostly senior adults at Community Church became concerned that the church was too program-driven. Many of them felt the church had lost the sense of community present in years past. They also felt that they were no longer an integral part of the larger church body. This group began to share their concerns with the senior pastor.

These sessions with the pastor resulted in a desire to restore a sense of family to the church fellowship. At first, people who were interested would meet for coffee after church and talk about the direction they wanted the church to go. After a couple of months, church members formed a family life committee to begin developing a family ministry program. The following suggestions may help you when forming a family life committee for your own church:

- Enlist eight to ten people.
- Choose people from all areas of church life.
- Include church leaders who can carry the vision to other areas of the church.

• Set aside two to six months to "dream" about becoming a family-powered church.

• Complete your time of "dreaming" with an overnight retreat to cement your ideas and develop a purpose statement.

LESSONS LEARNED

MAKE CHANGES SLOWLY

We will discuss shortly some of the ways to bring about change in an organization, but Community Church learned to enact change by thinking long-term and by moving slowly. This is especially important when you are attempting to completely change the way a church thinks about ministry. The members of Community Church were very intentional about the changes they made and refused to be motivated by a sense of urgency to move too quickly. As a result, they have experienced very few major obstacles along the way.

KEEP BASIC PRINCIPLES IN MIND

Community Church operated with two basic principles. The first principle was "Learn to think like a family." Though it's a simple idea, it is difficult to achieve. People reminded one another to "think like a family" as they discussed the changes they wanted to see.

The second principle was to "Evaluate the impact on families." Without necessarily implementing change, the family life committee, senior pastor, and staff evaluated current programs and events, as well as those being planned, for their impact—whether positive or negative—on families. These two principles served to remind church members of their desire to create a sense of family in the church.

ASK QUESTIONS

Community Church has developed three essential questions to guide the leadership and church fellowship toward the goal of a family-powered church. The questions are

• How do we, as a church, begin to think like a family?

- What does it mean for the church to be a family?
- How does what we do impact families—positively or negatively?

GOOD CHANGE HAPPENS IN STAGES

Community Church has been moving solidly in the direction of becoming a family-powered church for about three years. They are not yet where they want to be. But they have consistently moved ahead working toward long-term goals. Recognizing that opposition is often a consequence of inappropriate or abrupt change, this church has moved forward with the redirection of the church's ministry through a systematic approach to change.

FINE-TUNING CHANGES

Fine-tuning changes move us along in subtle, incremental steps that may not be noticeable to most people. For example, a church might begin to broaden the representation on committees of people with a passion for being a family of families. This can be done without much disruption when new people are regularly enlisted for committees.

ADJUSTMENT CHANGES

Adjustment changes are also incremental in nature, but they require larger adjustments. These changes may be noticeable to many people, but are usually easy to absorb into the life of the church. An example of this type of change would be consolidating meetings or eliminating unnecessary meetings in an effort to be more considerate of families. These types of changes will be felt by most people, but are not disruptive.

REORIENTATION CHANGES

Reorientation changes are long-term, strategic changes that radically redirect the church. These changes have great potential to be disruptive, particularly if they are initiated quickly and before significant fine-tuning and adjustment changes have occurred. Community Church is just beginning to implement reorientation changes, almost three years after the process was started.

START SMALL

As you begin to think about the steps your church might take in moving toward a family-powered church, you might consider some of the following suggestions.

- Consolidate or eliminate unnecessary meetings.
- Move meetings to just one night each week.
- Have people from different generations read morning Scripture.
- Model healthy family relationships.
- At times of new appointments, include individuals from different generations and people who have a passion for being a family of families.
- Begin to view the church as family.
- Plan one small multigenerational event.
- Look at one event each quarter and modify it as appropriate to make it a more family-powered event.
- When opportunities arise, talk with leadership about the importance of being a family of families.

Remember there is an essential theological and philosophical underpinning that should drive the way churches do ministry. Hopefully, the phrase "It is not about how we *do* ministry, it is about how we *think* ministry" has become a guiding principle for your church. Your challenge is to become a family of families, tied together in the unity of God's love.

"Therefore, as God's chosen people, holy and dearly loved, clothe yourselves with compassion, kindness, humility, gentleness and patience. Bear with each other, and forgive whatever grievances you may have against one another. Forgive as the Lord forgave you. And over all these virtues put on love, which binds them all together in perfect unity" (Colossians 3:12-14).

APPENDIX B: FAMILY MINISTRY PROGRAMMING

STORY-TIME MONTH

Each of these exercises is intended for families to build on what may have been taught in Sunday school or Bible study, either as parent-children times or children's study times. Parents can use these simple exercises for family devotions. For parents who do not have a regular devotion time, you might suggest that they replace one hour of television with one hour of devotions.

The information for each week's Story Time can be copied onto 8½x5½ sheets of cardstock. Adult leaders can prepare the cards ahead of time with the object attached or bring the printed cards to Bible study and allow the children to attach the object for that week.

Children who are too young to read the questions to parents can enlist the aid of older siblings or parents.

Week 1

Print the following guidelines on cardstock and attach a small bag of unpopped popcorn (microwave popcorn or sandwich bags with popcorn inside).

Instructions for parents

1. Pop the popcorn with your children, and add butter, salt, or other seasonings if you wish. Talk with your children about a time you made popcorn with your parents. Share with them how making popcorn nowadays is different from when you were a child (we now use hot-air poppers and microwaves—remember how cool we thought Jiffy Pop popcorn was?).

2. Sit down with your family in a comfortable spot to share the popcorn.

Instructions for children
Ask your parents the following questions:
1. Tell me about when I was born.
2. How did I get my name?
3. Where was I born?
4. Tell me about when you were born.
5. How did you get your name?

Instructions for parents
Wrap up your time together by reading Luke 1:26-33; 2:1-20. Ask your children what they find exciting about Jesus' birth. Tell them how important Jesus' name is and that Jesus means "the one who saves." Close in prayer thanking God for each member of your family and for Jesus.

Week 2
Print the following guidelines on cardstock and glue a small rock to the card.

Instructions for parents
Find a comfortable place outside to sit and talk. If possible, bring along some snacks.

Instructions for children
Ask your parents the following questions:
1. Tell me about a time things were really difficult for you and God provided.
2. Were you scared or frightened?
3. How did you know God was there for you?

Instructions for parents
Read Joshua 3:14–4:24 together. Ask the following questions:
1. What was the situation like for the Israelites?
2. How did God provide for them?
3. What did the rocks or stones stand for?

Tell your children that the rock on the card can remind them that God is always with us. Pray together thanking God for taking care of you.

Week 3

Print the following guidelines on cardstock. Make a puffy cloud with cotton balls and glue it to the card.

Instructions for parents
Find a comfortable place outside to sit and talk. If possible, bring some snacks.

Instructions for children
Ask your parents the following questions:
1. Tell me about someone who has been an inspiration to you.
2. Why is that person important to you?
3. Tell me about a special time you spent with that person.
Parents: You may want to talk about your grandfather who took you fishing, a good friend who taught you how to ride a bike, or your mother who was there for you when your dog died.

Instructions for parents
Point out an older adult (or several older adults) in your church family that your children could look up to. Tell your children why that person is special.
Read together Hebrews 12:1. Talk about what clouds do (e.g., provide rain as nourishment for plants and animals, provide snow and fun for skiers, provide shade to protect us from the hot sun). Talk about how big clouds are and how visible they are in the sky. Tell your children that God provides people in their lives who are "big" like clouds—people who can help us, protect us, have fun with us, teach us about things they have learned, and tell us they love us and that God loves us. Hebrews 12:1 tells us that these people are "witnesses." They tell us what they have experienced and what they have learned. Whenever we see a cloud we can remember that God provides witnesses for us. Pray together thanking God for the special people he has brought into our lives.

Week 4

Print the following guidelines on cardstock and attach a small heart-shaped cookie cutter to the card. Include a sugar cookie recipe on the back of the card.

Instructions for parents
Make the sugar cookies with your children. Answer the following questions while the cookies are baking.

Instructions for children
Ask your parents these questions:
1. What are three reasons you love me?
2. Tell me about someone or something you loved as a child.
3. What made that person or thing special?

Instructions for parents
Ask your children these questions:
1. What are some reasons you love me?
2. Tell me about someone or something you love (besides someone in the family).
3. What makes that person or thing special?
Read John 15:12 together. Talk about what it means that God loves you. Close in prayer thanking God for giving you parents, family, and others to love. Thank God for his love. Then share some cookies and milk with your family.

STEPS TO BEGIN A RITES-OF-PASSAGE PROGRAM

• Secure the support of church and family ministry leadership.

• Identify levels of responsibility to match each age you wish to mark with a rite of passage. (For example, you might want to celebrate various grade levels, such as seventh grade or twelfth grade. You may want to have four or five responsibilities to choose from for each age group.)

• Establish guidelines for participation at each level. (You might want to connect Bible study attendance or discipleship programs to participation in the rites of passage. You may want to have general guidelines for each age level and specific guidelines for specific tasks.)

EXAMPLES OF RITES OF PASSAGE FOR PARTICULAR AGE GROUPS

6th grade

Rite (or responsibility)

• Work alongside an adult in the nursery

• Pass out bulletins or programs for special events

Guidelines for participation

• Attend Bible study on a regular basis

• Attend training to be a nursery worker

7th grade

Rite (or responsibility)

• Serve as a "refreshment assistant" at vacation Bible school

• Assist visitors or senior adults in getting from the parking lot to worship service

Guidelines for participation

• Attend Bible study on a regular basis

• Meet with the VBS planning team for training as a refreshment assistant

• Meet with an adult in charge of greeting for training as a visitor's assistant

8th grade

Rite (or responsibility)
- Assist greeters on Sunday morning
- Serve as a game assistant during vacation Bible school

Guidelines for participation
- Attend Bible study on a regular basis
- Meet with an adult in charge of greeting for training
- Meet with the VBS game leader for training as a game assistant

9th grade

Rite (or responsibility)
- Participate in an adult worship team
- Read Scripture or prayer during Sunday morning worship

Guidelines for participation
- Attend Bible study on a regular basis
- Be regularly involved in small-group discipleship meetings
- Attend worship team practices

10th grade

Rite (or responsibility)
- Participate in the adult drama team

Guidelines for participation
- Attend Bible study on a regular basis
- Be active with a small-group discipleship team
- Attend drama team practices and meetings

11th grade

Rite (or responsibility)
- Be a teaching assistant in a preschool Sunday school class
- Mentor or tutor elementary-aged children

Guidelines for participation
- Attend Bible study on a regular basis
- Be involved in a small-group discipleship team
- Meet with the preschool teacher before becoming a teaching assistant
- Attend mentor or tutor training before tutoring

12th grade
Rite (or responsibility)
- Be a teaching assistant in a children's Sunday school class
- Participate in a church committee (e.g., the missions/outreach committee or family ministry committee)

Guidelines for participation
- Attend Bible study on a regular basis
- Be involved in a small-group discipleship team
- Meet with an adult teacher for planning meetings before serving as a teaching assistant
- Attend a training session with the senior pastor or member of the staff to participate in a church committee

FAMILY RENEWAL MONTH

Marion First Church of the Nazarene annually schedules a family renewal month which is called home improvement month. The example here reflects their emphasis on "home improvement."

ACTIVITIES SELECTED FOR THE MONTH

1. *Twelve hours of family prayer.* Family members are encouraged to come together for specific times of prayer during a given twelve-hour period on one Saturday during the month.

2. *A week of "TV fasting."* One week of the month is set aside for families to replace television, rented movies, and video games with other family-oriented activities. Families can sign up to accept the challenge. The church or the families might want to keep a chart of the hours "saved."

3. *Family-focused sermons.* Each week the sermon connects with the theme of family renewal.

4. *Family night at the "Y."* Plan a Saturday evening devoted to fun, food, and games held at the local YMCA. Usually churches can reserve space at the YMCA for a reasonable cost.

5. *Family progressive-game night.* Similar to a progressive dinner, groups of families play different board games. The rules of some games may have to be adjusted to accommodate family groups. Marion First Church has used games such as Blurt!, Outburst, Taboo, Beyond Balderdash, Pass the Pigs, Catch Phrase!, TriBond, Trivial Pursuit, and Pictionary. A specific time is allotted for each game and families are then moved to a different game site. Families will need to sign up ahead of time so that you can arrange the different teams. Leave extra spaces for families that do not sign up in advance. Be sure to promote this event throughout the entire church. Family teams of singles and/or members of other families can also participate. Encourage teams to enlist members of different ages. You may (or may not) decide to award points for the family winners of each game and award a grand prize at the end of the evening.

APPENDIX C: SAMPLE QUESTIONNAIRES

SHORT-FORM QUESTIONNAIRE

Describe your family context (check all that apply):

❏ Single parent and child(ren)
❏ Live alone
❏ Blended family
❏ Husband, wife, and child(ren)
❏ Live with roommate(s)
❏ More than two generations at home
❏ Close family members or friends nearby

Other/additional comments: _____

What are three things you like about your family?

1. _____
2. _____
3. _____

What are three strengths of your family?

1. _____
2. _____
3. _____

What are three things you would like to change about your family?

1. _____
2. _____
3. _____

How does church fellowship strengthen your family?

What programs or other opportunities would you like to see the church offer to help strengthen your family?

What are some of the issues you and/or your family are facing right now?

OUTREACH QUESTIONNAIRE

Describe your family context (check all that apply):

❑ Single parent and child(ren)
❑ Live alone
❑ Blended family
❑ Husband, wife, and child(ren)
❑ Live with roommate(s)
❑ More than two generations at home
❑ Close family members or friends nearby

Other/additional comments: _____

What are three things you like about your family?

1. _____
2. _____
3. _____

What are three strengths of your family?

1. _____
2. _____
3. _____

What are three things you would like to change about your family?

1. _____
2. _____
3. _____

What is your impression of our church?

In what ways could our church help your family?

What programs or other opportunities would you like to see the church offer to help strengthen you and your family?

What are some of the issues you and/or your family are facing right now?

QUESTIONNAIRE FOR ADOLESCENTS

Describe your family context (check all that apply):
- ❏ Single parent and child(ren)
- ❏ Blended family
- ❏ Dad, Mom, and child(ren)
- ❏ More than two generations at home
- ❏ Close family members or friends nearby

Other/additional comments: _____

What are three things you like about your family?
1. _____
2. _____
3. _____

What are three strengths of your family?
1. _____
2. _____
3. _____

What are three things you would like to change about your family?
1. _____
2. _____
3. _____

How does church fellowship strengthen your family?

What programs or other opportunities would you like to see the church offer to help strengthen your family?

What are some of the issues you and/or your family are facing right now?

How can the church pray for you or minister to you?

IN-DEPTH QUESTIONNAIRE

Describe your family context (check all that apply):
☐ Single parent and child(ren)
☐ Live alone
☐ Blended family
☐ Husband, wife, and child(ren)
☐ Live with roommate(s)
☐ More than two generations at home
☐ Close family members or friends nearby

Other/additional comments: _____
Ages of adults: _____
Ages of children: _____

What are three things you like about your family?
1. _____
2. _____
3. _____

What are three strengths of your family?
1. _____
2. _____
3. _____

What are three things you would like to change about your family?
1. _____
2. _____
3. _____

How does church fellowship strengthen your family?

What programs or other opportunities would you like to see the church offer to help strengthen your family?

What are some of the issues you and/or your family are facing right now?

Please mark the top five concerns for your *family*:

___ alcohol or drugs

___ schoolwork/homework

___ communication

___ relationships with other
      family members

___ discipline

___ self-esteem

___ faith in Christ

___ sexuality

___ friends

___ stress

___ knowledge of Scriptures

___ violence

___ loneliness/isolation

___ managing finances

___ spiritual growth

___ time management

Other: _____

Please mark *your* top five concerns:

___ alcohol or drugs	___ friends
___ new stage in life	___ stress
___ communication	___ knowledge of Scriptures
___ relationships with other family members	___ violence
	___ loneliness/isolation
___ work situation	___ managing finances
___ self-esteem	___ spiritual growth
___ faith in Christ	___ time management
___ sexuality	___ dating issues

Other: _____

Please mark the top five concerns for your *marriage* (if applicable):

___ alcohol or drugs	___ knowledge of Scriptures
___ new stage in life	___ violence
___ communication	___ loneliness/isolation
___ relationships with other family members	___ managing finances
	___ spiritual growth
___ work situation	___ time management
___ self-esteem	___ understanding personality differences
___ faith in Christ	
___ sexuality	___ understanding needs and expectations of spouse
___ friends	
___ stress	___ intimacy

Other: _____

APPENDIX D:
RECOMMENDED RESOURCES

FAMILY MINISTRY RESOURCES

Resources on Contemporary Families

Beyond Chaos: Living the Christian Family in a World Like Ours, Chris William Erdman. Grand Rapids, MI: William B. Eerdmans Publishing Company, 1996. This resource examines the implications for families living in our contemporary culture. Specifically, this book focuses on how Christian families can "live in the world...but not be of the world..."

Families at the Crossroads: Beyond Traditional and Modern Options, Rodney Clapp. Downers Grove, IL: InterVarsity Press, 1993. Clapp discusses his understanding of a theology of church and a theology of family in light of the broad spectrum of contemporary philosophies on the Christian family. This book will motivate you to think about your own understanding of family and church.

The Family: A Christian Perspective on the Contemporary Home, Jack O. Balswick and Judith K. Balswick. Grand Rapids, MI: Baker Book House, 1999. This book examines the theological foundations for family along with several key issues for healthy families including communication, sexuality, and marriage.

The Family Covenant: Love and Forgiveness in the Christian Home, Dennis B. Guernsey. Pasadena, CA: Hope Publishing House, 1999. This book looks scripturally at what it means for families to be in a covenant relationship.

Life After Divorce, Bobbie Reed. St. Louis, MO: Concordia Publishing House, 1993. This practical handbook covers the different stages of divorce.

The Shelter of Each Other: Rebuilding Our Families, Mary Pipher. New York, NY: Ballantine Books, 1997. Pipher assesses the stressors on contemporary families and provides helpful insights into how we can strengthen the family.

Ties That Stress: The New Family Imbalance, David Elkind. Cambridge, MA: Harvard University Press, 1995. A helpful resource in understanding the impact of societal changes on the dynamics of family life.

The Way We Never Were: American Families and the Nostalgia Trap, Stephanie Coontz. New York, NY: Basic Books, 2000. Coontz offers a comprehensive look at the history of the American family, separating myth from reality.

The Way We Really Are: Coming to Terms with America's Changing Families, Stephanie Coontz. New York, NY: Basic Books, 1998. Coontz examines the realities of contemporary families, looking at how factors such as divorce, single parenting, and two-income families impact our lives.

Resources for Parents

101 Things You Can Do for Our Children's Future, Richard Louv. New York, NY: Anchor Books/Doubleday, 1994.

501 Practical Ways to Love Your Husband and Kids, Jennifer Baker. St. Louis, MO: Concordia Publishing House, 1996.

501 Practical Ways to Love Your Wife and Kids, Roger Sonnenberg. St. Louis, MO: Concordia Publishing House, 1996.

Celebrate Home: Great Ideas for Stay-at-Home Moms, Angie Peters. St. Louis, MO: Concordia Publishing House, 1998.

Christian Parenting: Raising Children in the Real World, Donna Sinclair and Yvonne Stewart. Louisville, KY: Westminster John Knox Press, 1992.

Family Tales: Rewriting the Stories That Made You Who You Are, James Osterhaus. Downers Grove, IL: InterVarsity Press, 1997. A good reference on storytelling and ritual. Through our family stories we can better know ourselves, our dreams, and our struggles.

How to Parent Your "Tweenager": Understanding the In-Between Years of Your 8 to 12 Year Old, Dr. Mary Manz Simon. Nashville, TN: Thomas Nelson Publishers, 1995.

How to Risk-Proof Your Kids, Kathleen Winkler. St. Louis, MO: Concordia Publishing House, 1996. This book contains information to help parents guide their children in making wise decisions.

Imagine That!: 365 Wacky Ways to Build a Creative Christian Family, Mike and Amy Nappa. Minneapolis, MN: Augsburg Fortress Publishing, 1998. This book is full of simple ideas designed to get families together and talking to each other.

John Rosemond's Six-Point Plan for Raising Happy, Healthy Children, John K. Rosemond. Kansas City, MO: Andrews and McMeel, 1989. Rosemond asserts that any parent, whatever the context, can raise happy, well-adjusted children by following his six-step plan. A very helpful resource.

Lessons in Dadhood From the Father Who Really Knows Best, Tim Wesemann. St. Louis, MO: Concordia Publishing House, 1997. Practical devotions specifically directed at fathers.

Renewing the Family Spirit: Overcoming Conflict to Enjoy Stronger Family Ties, David J. Ludwig. St. Louis, MO: Concordia Publishing House, 1989. This book discusses the spiritual influences in our homes and highlights ways to create a better home life.

Surviving Your Child's Dating Years: 7 Vital Skills That Help Your Child Build Healthy Relationships, Bobbie Reed. St. Louis, MO: Concordia Publishing House, 1996. This book offers seven skills essential to help parents prepare their children for dating.

Understanding Today's Youth Culture, Walt Mueller. Wheaton, IL: Tyndale House Publishers, Inc., 1999. Written for parents and for youth workers, this book provides very practical insight into today's adolescent culture.

Resources for Grandparents

Grandparenting by Grace: A Guide Through the Joys and Struggles, Irene M. Endicott. Nashville, TN: Broadman & Holman Publishers, 1994. This twelve-week study helps grandparents discover their potential to impact their families spiritually and emotionally and how they can leave a legacy for their children and grandchildren.

Innovative Grandparenting, Karen O'Connor. St. Louis, MO: Concordia Publishing House, 1996. This book provides valuable information to help grandparents build memorable relationships with their grandchildren.

Books for Children

501 Practical Ways to Love Your Grandparents, Roger Sonnenberg, et al. St. Louis, MO: Concordia Publishing House, 1999.

Comforting Little Hearts Series, Robin Prince Monroe. St. Louis, MO: Concordia Publishing House, 1998. A series of books for children that helps them deal with some of the difficult issues they might face (including *Why Don't We Live Together Anymore?: Understanding Divorce* and *I Have a New Family Now: Understanding Blended Families*).

What Happened When Grandma Died, Peggy Barker. St. Louis, MO: Concordia Publishing House, 1984.

Resources for Pastors

The Complete Handbook for Family Life Ministry in the Church, Don W. Hebbard and H. Norman Wright. Nashville, TN: Thomas Nelson Publishers, 1995. A practical, step-by-step guide for developing a family ministry.

Faith Traditions and the Family, Phyllis D. Airhart and Margaret Lamberts Bendroth, editors. Louisville, KY: Westminster John Knox Press, 1996. This book examines eleven different faith traditions and how each of these traditions interacts with the family.

Family-Centered Church: A New Parish Model, Gerald Foley. Kansas City, MO: Sheed & Ward (BookMasters), 1995.

The Family-Friendly Church, Ben Freudenburg and Rick Lawrence. Loveland, CO: Group Publishing, Inc., 1998. This book contains helpful suggestions and takes you on Freudenburg's journey of discovering the importance of family ministry.

Family Ministry, Second Edition, Charles M. Sell. Grand Rapids, MI: Zondervan Publishing House, 1995. Sell presents a thorough study of the issues surrounding family ministry and ways that church can implement a healthy, vibrant ministry.

Generation to Generation: Family Process in Church and Synagogue, Edwin H. Friedman. New York, NY: Guilford Publications, 1985. This book is a helpful resource for pastors seeking to adopt a "church as family" model of ministry.

Resources for Youth Pastors

130 Ways to Involve Parents in Youth Ministry. Loveland, CO: Group Publishing, Inc., 1994. This book is a compilation of ideas from youth ministers throughout the U.S. that will help you get parents involved in your youth ministry.

Family-Based Youth Ministry: Reaching the Been-There, Done That Generation, Mark DeVries. Downers Grove, IL: InterVarsity Press, 1994. An excellent resource that provides an in-depth study of the issues surrounding ministry to families of adolescents.

New Directions for Youth Ministry. Loveland, CO: Group Publishing, Inc., 1998. Chapter 3, "Reconstructing Family Life," provides a model of youth ministry that partners with the extended church and families to reach young people.

Tag-Team Youth Ministry: 50 Ways to Involve Parents and Other Caring Adults, Ron Habermas and David Olshine. Cincinnati, OH: Standard Publishing Company, 1995.

The Youth Worker's Handbook to Family Ministry: Strategies and Practical Ideas for Reaching Your Students' Families, Chap Clark. Grand Rapids, MI: Zondervan Publishing House, 1997. This book provides a very basic framework within which to assess the youth pastor's ministry to families of adolescents. It is also a helpful resource for any pastor interested in family ministry.

Family Devotions

A Family Garden of Christian Virtues, Susan Lawrence. St. Louis, MO: Concordia Publishing House, 1997.

Family Time Fun: Great Stuff to Do With Your Kids, Elizabeth Friedrich. St. Louis, MO: Concordia Publishing House, 1994. Devotions coupled with activities for parents with young children.

Fun Excuses to Talk About God (book and discussion guide), Joani Schultz. Loveland, CO: Group Publishing, Inc., 1997.

Laugh and Tickle, Hug and Pray: Active Family Devotions, Julaine Kammrath. St. Louis, MO: Concordia Publishing House, 1997. A collection of fifty-two stories designed to get parents and children talking together.

Little Visits for Families, Allan Hart Jahsmann and Martin P. Simon. St. Louis, MO: Concordia Publishing House, 1997.

A Young Child's Garden of Christian Virtues: Imaginative Ways to Plant God's Word in Toddlers' Hearts, Susan Lawrence. St. Louis, MO: Concordia Publishing House, 1998.

Activities for Families at Church

Affordable Family Fun: Family Fun for Under $5, Susan L. Lingo. Loveland, CO: Group Publishing, Inc., 1998. This book offers inexpensive, creative ideas for getting families together.

Family-Friendly Ideas Your Church Can Do. Loveland, CO: Group Publishing, Inc., 1998. Fifty creative ways to bring families together including family service projects and worship services. Very practical.

Fun Ideas for the Family-Friendly Church. Loveland, CO: Group Publishing, Inc., 2000.

Funtastic Family Nights, Kurt Bickel. St. Louis, MO: Concordia Publishing House, 1998. This book offers nineteen practical ideas for family night programs.

Periodicals

Christian Parenting Today, Christianity Today. For Christian parents with children of all ages.

HomeLife, LifeWay Resources. For families with children of all ages.

Living With Teenagers, LifeWay Resources. A resource for parents of adolescents.

ParentLife, LifeWay Resources. Offers a Christian perspective for parents of preschoolers and other children.

ParentLife Newborn Edition, LifeWay Resources. Special annual edition of ParentLife magazine for parents of newborns.

Rev., Group Publishing, Inc. Includes a column about family ministry in each issue.

Curriculum Resources for Families

Covenant Marriage: Communication and Intimacy (leader guide and couple's guide), Gary Chapman and Betty Hassler. LifeWay Resources (www.bssb.com). Twelve-session study designed to equip couples to achieve responsible communication and intimacy in their marriages.

Covenant Marriage: Partnership and Commitment (leader guide and couple's guide), Diana Garland and Betty Hassler. LifeWay Resources (www.bssb.com). Twelve-session study to teach married couples sharing and communication skills.

Counsel for the Nearly and Newly Married (leader guide and couple's guide), Ernest White and James E. White. LifeWay Resources (www.bssb.com). This series focuses on enriching couple's relationships.

Empowered Parenting: Raising Kids in the Nurture and Instruction of the Lord, Robert J. Morgan. LifeWay Resources (www.bssb.com). An eight-session study that offers parenting skills from a biblically focused point of view.

FaithWeaver™ Bible Curriculum, Group Publishing, Inc., (www.faithweaver.com). In this curriculum, all age levels study the same Bible point at the same time within a Christian education program.

Getting Along With Parents, Group's Active Bible Curriculum, Senior High. Group Publishing, Inc., (www.grouppublishing.com).

Getting Along With Your Family, Group's Active Bible Curriculum, Senior High. Group Publishing, Inc., (www.grouppublishing.com).

I Take Thee to Be My Spouse: Bible Study for Newlyweds, David Apple. LifeWay Resources (www.bssb.com). Bible study designed to equip newlyweds with the necessary skills to enter into a marriage covenant.

KidShare: What Do I Do Now? (facilitator guide and member book), Cindy Pitts. LifeWay Resources (www.bssb.com). This twelve-session study is designed for children whose parents have divorced or remarried.

Making Love Last Forever Leader Kit, Gary Smalley. LifeWay Resources (www.bssb.com). Twelve-week study designed to help couples understand how to foster a love relationship.

New Faces in the Frame: A Guide to Marriage and Parenting in the Blended Family, Dick Dunn. LifeWay Resources (www.bssb.com). Two six-week studies designed to help people develop skills to succeed as a blended family.

Parenting by Grace: Discipline and Spiritual Growth, (leader guide and member book), Dixie R. Crase and Arthur H. Criscoe. LifeWay Resources (www.bssb.com). A ten-week study that helps parents understand how to love, affirm, and discipline their children in the context of God's grace.

Peace in the Family: A Home Activity Book, William Mitchell and Mikey Thomas Oldham. LifeWay Resources (www.bssb.com). This workbook teaches families basic conflict resolution skills.

Prayer in the Family: A Home Activity Book, William Mitchell and Cindy Pitts. LifeWay Resources (www.bssb.com). A thirty-day adventure to help families build an effective prayer life into their daily routine.

Self-Control in the Family: A Home Activity Book, William Mitchell and Phyllis Belew. LifeWay Resources (www.bssb.com). This workbook is designed to help families become more disciplined.

Strengthening Family Relationships, Apply-It-To-Life™ Adult Bible Curriculum. Group Publishing, Inc., (www.grouppublishing.com).

A Time for Healing: Coming to Terms with Your Divorce (facilitator guide and book), Harold Ivan Smith. LifeWay Resources (www.bssb.com). This study helps adults work through a variety of issues stemming from divorce.

The Truth About Our Families, Core Belief Bible Study Series for Middle School/Junior High. Group Publishing, Inc., (www.grouppublishing.com).

Why Our Families Matter, Core Belief Bible Study Series for Senior High. Group Publishing, Inc., (www.grouppublishing.com).

Video Resources

Building Strong Families Leader Kit, Bill Mitchell. LifeWay Resources (www.bssb.com). Focuses on parental leadership, characteristics of strong families, and developing biblical character.

The Five Love Languages Video Pack, Gary Chapman. LifeWay Resources (www.bssb.com). Video pack for couples which includes *The Five Love Languages Viewer Guide* and *The Five Love Languages* book.

The Five Love Languages of Children Video Pack, Gary Chapman and Ross Campbell. LifeWay Resources (www.bssb.com). Video pack to help parents learn their child's "primary love language." Contains the book *The Five Love Languages of Children.*

Parenting With Purpose Kit, Roger Sonnenberg. Concordia Publishing House (www.cph.org). Focuses on strengthening families in the areas of communication, developing a strong faith, and strengthening personal relationships, this video curriculum helps parents incorporate healthy characteristics of families into their daily lives.

Parenting With Values Kit, Roger Sonnenberg. Concordia Publishing House (www.cph.org). A six-session video resource to help parents teach the values that they want to pass on to their children.

The Power of We: God's Gift to Marriage Kit, David Ludwig. Concordia Publishing House (www.cph.org). Video curriculum designed to help couples understand various issues of marriage.

Shaping the Next Generation Leader Kit, David and Elaine Atchison. LifeWay Resources (www.bssb.com). Video sessions designed to give parents basic information and tools necessary to shape the spiritual character of their children.

Understanding Your Teenager Video Curriculum, Wayne Rice and Ken Davis. Zondervan Publishing House/Youth Specialties (www.zondervan.com). This resource provides valuable insights for parents into the typical developmental issues facing adolescents and for how parents might better be equipped to help their children navigate these years.

Group Publishing, Inc.
Attention: Product Development
P.O. Box 481
Loveland, CO 80539
Fax: (970) 679-4370

Evaluation for
The Family-Powered Church

Please help Group Publishing, Inc., continue to provide innovative and useful resources for ministry. Please take a moment to fill out this evaluation and mail or fax it to us. Thanks!

● ● ●

1. As a whole, this book has been (circle one)

not very helpful   very helpful

1   2   3   4   5   6   7   8   9   10

2. The best things about this book:

3. Ways this book could be improved:

4. Things I will change because of this book:

5. Other books I'd like to see Group publish in the future:

6. Would you be interested in field-testing future Group products and giving us your feedback? If so, please fill in the information below:

Name_____

Church Name _____

Denomination _____ Church Size _____

Church Address _____

City _____ State _____ ZIP _____

Church Phone _____

E-mail _____

Exciting Resources for Pastors and Church Leaders

AquaChurch: Essential Leadership Arts for Piloting Your Church in Today's Fluid Culture

Leonard Sweet

In this latest and most accessible work from church historian, futurist and best-selling author Leonard Sweet, church leaders will discover the leadership arts that are essential in today's ever-changing culture. The author provides thought-provoking yet practical skills that will elevate the scope of ministry from mere survival of daily challenges to thriving in today's culture! Rather than provide new maps that will soon be obsolete, this book illustrates the need to become an "AquaChurch" in order to effectively minister in a fluid, postmodern culture.

ISBN 0-7644-2151-4

Experience God in Worship

Discover the look of worship in the 21st century! Find out what thriving churches are doing, what changes they're planning, and how your church can make worship a joyful celebration all year long! You'll hear from nationally recognized authorities George Barna, Gary M. Burge, Richard Allen Farmer, Jack W. Hayford, Kim Hill, Bruce H. Leafblad, John S. Miller, Leonard Sweet, and Robert Webber. Whether your church is evangelical, African-American, liturgical, charismatic, contemporary or something in-between, you'll gain insight into current trends, lasting traditions, and more.

ISBN 0-7644-2133-6

The Dirt on Learning

Thom & Joani Schultz

This thought-provoking book, from veteran educators Thom & Joani Schultz, explores what Jesus' Parable of the Sower says about effective teaching and learning. Readers will rethink the Christian education methods used in their churches and consider what really works. While this book issues a direct challenge—to evaluate the effectiveness of a church's Christian education program—the tone is reassuring and positive. Implementing the authors' proposals will increase the impact of any Christian education program—and make a lifelong difference in the lives of learners.

Book Only   ISBN 0-7644-2088-7

The Dirt on Learning Video Training Kit

With this video training kit, churches can train their entire staff. Includes the book, training video, 12 overhead transparencies, a leader's guide with reproducible handouts, seed packets, magazine subscription discounts and more!

ISBN 0-7644-2152-2

The Family-Friendly Church

Ben Freudenburg with Rick Lawrence

This book is a must-have for every church leader! Discover how certain programming can often short-circuit your church's ability to truly strengthen families—and what you can do about it! You'll get practical ideas and suggestions featuring profiles of real churches. It also includes thought-provoking application worksheets that will help you apply the principles and insights to your own church.

ISBN 0-7644-2048-8